Using the Learning Cycle to Teach Physical Science

Using the Learning Cycle to Teach Physical Science

A Hands-on Approach for the Middle Grades

Paul C. Beisenherz
and
Marylou Dantonio

Heinemann
Portsmouth, NH

Heinemann
A division of Reed Elsevier Inc.
361 Hanover Street
Portsmouth, NH 03801–3912
Offices and agents throughout the world

Library of Congress Cataloging-in-Publication Data

Beisenherz, Paul C.
    Using the learning cycle to teach physical science : a hands-on
approach for the middle grades / Paul C. Beisenherz and Marylou
Dantonio.
        p.   cm.
    Includes bibliographical references and index.
    ISBN 0–435–08376–7
    1. Physical sciences—Study and teaching (Secondary) 2. Learning.
I. Dantonio, Marylou. II. Title.
Q181.B438 1996
500.2'071'2—dc20   95–24856
                                                       CIP

Editor: Leigh Peake
Production: J. B. Tranchemontagne
Manufacturing: Louise Richardson
Design: Catherine Hawkes
Cover Design: Barbara Whitehead

Printed in the United States of America on acid-free paper
99 98 97 96 VG 9 8 7 6 5 4 3 2 1

CONTENTS

Contents

INTRODUCTION

Do you find science fun and exciting to learn and teach? How comfortable are you teaching science? How confident? If you have doubts about your ability to present an exciting and stimulating science program, you are not alone! The many studies of science teaching over the past decade have shown that there are major problems with how, and how much, science is being taught in elementary and middle schools. In schools that do not specifically designate science periods, the physical sciences in particular receive short shrift. The little science that is taught is mostly without benefit of hands-on, concrete activities or the use of inquiry. Instead, curriculum guides emphasize science facts and vocabulary.

This book takes a very different approach to teaching science. It makes science more exciting for students by enabling them to construct and apply basic science concepts. This develops thinking skills. In addition, the learning cycle approach found in this book conveys a more accurate view of science—as a process of inquiry rather than a body of knowledge.

Teachers whose models of teaching science include many of the strategies and techniques found here will be challenged to fine-tune their teaching and identify additional activities to supplement their curriculum.

The Learning Cycle Strategy enables students themselves to construct discrete science concepts. It includes an Exploration Phase, in which students are exposed to hands-on activities; an Introduction Phase, in which the concept is formally introduced; and an Application Phase, in which the concept is reinforced and expanded through additional experiences. All phases of the Learning Cycle use teacher questions to guide the learning experience.

In their review of studies involving learning cycle approaches, Lawson, Abraham, and Renner (1989) state that "the learning cycle approach appears to have considerable promise in areas of encouraging positive attitudes toward science and science instruction, developing better content achievement by students, and improving general thinking skills" (69).

Suppose that next Monday you are to introduce your students to the concept: Air expands when it is heated and contracts when it is cooled. In preparing to teach this concept, your answers to the following questions will significantly affect your presentation:

1. Why have you chosen to teach this concept? What goals and objectives do you want to achieve through your lesson?
2. What instructional strategies will most effectively allow your students to construct the concept that temperature affects the expansion and contraction of air and provide the highest possible motivational climate?
3. What questioning techniques will help your students construct the concept and develop scientific thinking?

> **Students do not simply learn what is taught. Rather, their experiences modify prior beliefs, yielding a scientific knowledge that is uniquely personal. Learning takes place when students construct their own representation of knowledge. Facts and formulas will not become part of deep intuition if they are only committed to memory. They must be explored, used, revised, tested, modified, and finally accepted through a process of active investigation, argument, and participation. Science instruction that does not provide these types of opportunities rarely achieves its objectives.**
>
> **—L. A. Steen**

Section I discusses these important questions and develops a rationale for the Learning Cycle as an effective way to teach science concepts. Section II includes six basic physical science concepts that are common to most middle school science curricula. Each Learning Cycle centers on a single concept or idea and includes a number of sequenced, hands-on activities presented as a Learning Cycle.

Each activity is student-directed and

▼ identifies a problem focus
▼ lists the materials required by each student or student group
▼ suggests a procedure for resolving the identified problem
▼ delineates key questions teachers can use to prompt the appropriate thinking processes
▼ includes teacher background information regarding content, needed skills or recipes, and pedagogical considerations.

In addition, each Learning Cycle begins with a brief introduction to the content topic, a discussion of the Learning Cycle Strategy developed for that content topic, mention of safety considerations and supply sources, and a list of related reference materials.

Section III is a unique opportunity for you to develop your own Learning Cycle Sequence. It contains randomly sequenced activities related to the concept of surface tension. Using these activities and others you may create, you can construct your own Learning Cycle Sequence, applying what you have learned in Sections I and II.

We hope this book encourages you to rethink your personal model for teaching science, allowing the strategies found here—which have been shown to motivate students and help them develop science concepts, thinking skills, and a scientific attitude—to challenge your thinking. Your initial exposure to these strategies should be in an environment that will allow you every opportunity to succeed. By applying the techniques used in this book to the topics found in your own curriculum, we hope that you will become, in a sense, renewed, incorporating strategies such as the Learning Cycle into your personal model for teaching science.

To modify your personal model takes time, energy, and, most importantly, commitment. As you use a Learning Cycle approach with hands-on activities and incorporate other instructional techniques into your teaching, you will gain confidence in your ability to teach science and experience the personal satisfaction of observing highly motivated students in your class.

REFERENCES

Glascow, D.R. 1983. "Identifying the Real Elementary Science Curriculum." *Science and Children* 20 (8): 56–59.

Lawson, A.E., Abraham, M.R., and Renner, J.W. 1989. *A Theory of Instruction: Using the Learning Cycle to Teach Science Concepts and Thinking Skills.* National Association for Research in Science Teaching (NARST) Monograph Number One.

Mechling, K.R., and Oliver, D.L. 1983. *What Research Says about Elementary School Science* (Handbook IV). Washington, D.C.: National Science Teachers Association.

Pratt, H. 1981. "Science Education in the Elementary School." In *What Research Says to the Science Teacher,* Volume 3, ed. Harms, N.C., and Yager, R.E. Washington, D.C.: National Science Teachers Association.

Steen, L.A. 1991. "Reaching for Science Literacy." *Change* 23 (4):10–19.

THE LEARNING CYCLE
STRATEGY

WHY TEACH SCIENCE?

Every teacher has his or her own goals for teaching science. For some, covering the textbook or locally developed program fulfills school and/or school district goals. For others, these curricular goals are embellished by goals such as developing curiosity or student independence and autonomy that are personally felt by the teacher to be important for their students.

An effective science program demands that teachers and administrators share a high degree of commitment to the goals of the program. It is helpful to think through what you would like students to be able to do when they have finished the program. What behaviors should they be able to demonstrate? Here are some of the goals that underlie the approach to science instruction described in this book.

1. Students should be able to think scientifically. In practicing the methods of science, students will not only better understand the nature of science and how it works but also develop thinking skills that will increase their ability to solve problems.

   While promoting scientific thinking has long been a goal for science teaching, an early sixties elementary school science program, *Science: A Process Approach* (SAPA), supported by the National Science Foundation and the American Association for the Advancement of Science, provided a national focus for defining and using thinking skills in science classes. The developers of this program identified thinking as a number of "process skills"—for example, observing, ordering, inferring, applying—that correspond to the thinking skills scientists use to solve problems. Authors of science textbooks, state and local science curriculum guides, and other resources for science teachers have incorporated many of these process skills into their goals, objectives, and activities.

   The process skills involved in each activity are identified by key questions in parentheses. Daily reinforcement of process skills makes your students more aware of the thinking processes they are using to solve problems.

2. Students should be able to demonstrate that they are curious, tolerant of ambiguity and frustration, open-minded, and willing to suspend judgment. These qualities are important aspects of a scientific attitude.

3. Students should be able to demonstrate increased autonomy and independence in their investigation of problems.

4. Students should perceive themselves as highly capable of learning about science. They should *expect* to succeed in tasks assigned to them during science time.

5. Students should demonstrate an interest in a wide variety of science topics. One of the most important goals we can have as teachers of science is to make every topic we teach as exciting and motivating as possible for our students.

6. Students should experience opportunities to test out and discover limitations in their personal beliefs and in their understanding of their world.

7. Students should experience a rich collection of concrete experiences related to a list of basic science topics identified by the school or school district. In order to help our students construct more "accurate" science concepts from their existing preconceptions and misconceptions, they must be exposed to appropriate concrete experiences.

8. Students should be able to carry over their science process skills to other school subjects—reading, mathematics, and social studies, for example.

These outcomes resoundingly justify science as a high priority in our schools. We desperately need motivated, curious students who can think, withhold judgment, tolerate ambiguity, and can work independently to solve problems.

Specific strategies to help our students achieve these goals

A number of research efforts clearly indicate that activity-centered, hands-on science experiences can help teachers achieve the above goals. Shymansky and his colleagues (1982) summarize their review of hands-on science programs by stating that students in hands-on science curricula "achieved more, liked science more, and improved their skills more than did students in traditional, textbook-based classrooms" (15). Because hands-on science does not depend heavily on reading skills, poor readers and other special students are better able to succeed. In addition, there is considerable evidence that the use of an activity-centered science program enhances reading readiness and math skills (Mechling and Oliver 1983).

The real question then is not whether to use an activity-centered approach but rather how to package the hands-on experiences for the students' greatest benefit. The Learning Cycle approach used to develop each content topic in this book is a highly effective strategy for organizing hands-on science instruction. In addition to being activity-oriented, it allows teachers to develop science concepts, identify and sequence effective questions, motivate students, manage students and materials, and assess student understanding of and attitudes toward science instruction.

WHAT IS A LEARNING CYCLE STRATEGY?

The Learning Cycle, an increasingly popular strategy for teaching science concepts, has its roots in the Science Curriculum Improvement Study (SCIS), an NSF-sponsored elementary science program developed in the 1960s (Karplus and Thier 1967).

In essence, the strategy uses questions, activities, experiences, and examples to prompt students in developing a science concept, reinforcing their understanding of the concept, and applying the concept to new situations.

Renner and Marek (1988) provide an excellent rationale and justification for using Learning Cycles. They relate a Learning Cycle approach to the nature of science:

> A Learning Cycle comes from the discipline itself; it represents science. If science is to be taught in a manner that leads students to construct knowledge, they must make a quest. The Learning Cycle leads students on that quest for knowledge (170).

Besides being a sound instructional strategy for formulating science concepts, a Learning Cycle can be a useful tool to help your students to define science as a process of inquiry rather than as a body of knowledge. It is an excellent opportunity for students to understand and use the science processes: observing, comparing and contrasting, ordering, categorizing, relating, inferring, communicating, and applying. These processes are defined in Science Framework for California Public Schools (1990) as "mental functions that suggest the dynamic, higher-level effort required in thinking scientifically" (144).

An important part of a Learning Cycle strategy is carefully planned questioning sequences. All the activities in Section II include questions that initiate and guide science processes. The kind of science processes required by each question is identified in parentheses.

Phases of a Learning Cycle

A Learning Cycle is a three-phased sequence: Exploration, Concept Introduction, and Application.

Exploration.   At the beginning of a Learning Cycle, students explore new materials, phenomena, problems, and ideas using direct experiences to make observations and collect data. For many concepts, the Exploration Phase begins with less structured opportunities for students to explore objects and systems at their own pace with little guidance from you. Then, more structured exploratory experiences help students reexamine the same objects, systems, and preconceptions more scientifically (Barnes, Shaw, and Spector 1989). For some concepts, you may minimize the less structured experiences and ask your students to identify and compare similarities observed among a more structured sequence of experiences. In either case, these experiences and discussions guide students to understanding a concept. Although students should *not* be formally introduced to the concept or terminology that is being developed during the Exploration Phase, they *do* need to be aware of any essential prerequisite concepts, skills, and techniques.

During the Exploration Phase, you should identify students' preconceptions and misconceptions about the concept by asking students to perform a hands-on activity and then listening carefully as they explain their observations. By assessing your students' preconceptions and misconceptions, you can then select and sequence activities to help them construct a more accurate explanation of the phenomena. The Learning Cycles in Section II suggest a sequence of activities for teaching each concept. You may need to alter that sequence as you assess students' questions and responses.

The number of activities in the Exploration Phase will vary with the nature of the concept and with the students. Generally, you need enough examples to enable students to identify common attributes or characteristics; this will help them describe and define the concept being developed. If a lot of your students cannot identify the common characteristics of the activities you've had them perform, then you'll need to let them explore additional activities. The hands-on activities students perform during the Exploration Phase of a Learning Cycle are an important source of motivation. Because students experience these activities *before* the concept is introduced, they are actively generating questions and searching for and testing hypotheses to explain their observations (Brooks and Brooks 1993). Each exploration activity has a problem focus that should grab students' interest and arouse their curiosity.

Typically, this kind of motivation is missing in traditional textbooks. Instead, students are aware of the concept *before* they do a hands-on activity—through the text, the pictures, or a lecture. Sometimes even the title of the hands-on activity itself identifies the concept to be investigated. As a result, there is no problem focus, and little curiosity, puzzlement, or interest is generated.

We must design our instruction so that students are pursuing solutions to real problems of real interest to them. We miss a significant source of motivation if we do not include an Exploration Phase for the science concepts we teach.

Concept Introduction.   In this phase, the scientific concept that describes or explains what the students have observed is introduced in scientific vocabulary appropriate for your students. Together, your students and you organize the observations and experiences noted during the Exploration Phase. Often the patterns identified match the concept of the lesson. Conversations among your students and between your students and you can help you see how the newly acquired information has affected the students' mental constructions of the concept. You can then use the textbook, audiovisual aids, and other materials to explain the concept further. Introducing the concept should serve as a framework from which further discoveries can be made—not a conclusion or wrapping up of the Exploration Phases observations.

Application.   During this phase, give your students new examples of problems (often in the form of additional hands-on activities) that reinforce, extend, or expand the concept. This phase gives your students time and opportunities to incorporate the concept into their thinking. This is especially valuable for those students who tend to process information more slowly and who therefore may not yet be able to communicate their understanding of the concept.

The diagram below depicts the flow of a Learning Cycle schematically. In some cases, one or more of the activities in the application phase of one Learning Cycle can serve either to expand the concept by identifying additional attributes of the concept, or to provide the initial activity in the Exploration Phase of a new, closely related concept.

In Section II, Learning Cycle 2—Acids and Bases—and Learning Cycle 3—Properties of Carbon Dioxide—are excellent examples of the potential relationship between two Learning Cycle sequences. The last activity in the Application Phase of the acids/bases sequence serves as the first activity in the Exploration Phase of the properties of carbon dioxide sequence. Likewise, the last activity in the Application Phase of the circuit sequence (Learning Cycle 5) could serve as the first activity in the Exploration Phase of a new Learning Cycle on conductors of electricity.

The hands-on activities in the Application Phase can be a source of additional motivation. By again encountering a problem focus for each activity, students can apply their newly acquired concept to new situations—reinforcing and extending their understanding of the concept and increasing the likelihood that their understanding of the concept will be accurate. This has the added benefit of increasing self-esteem.

You can also select some activities from the Application Phase that will extend the concept beyond science into other areas (like art, language arts, or

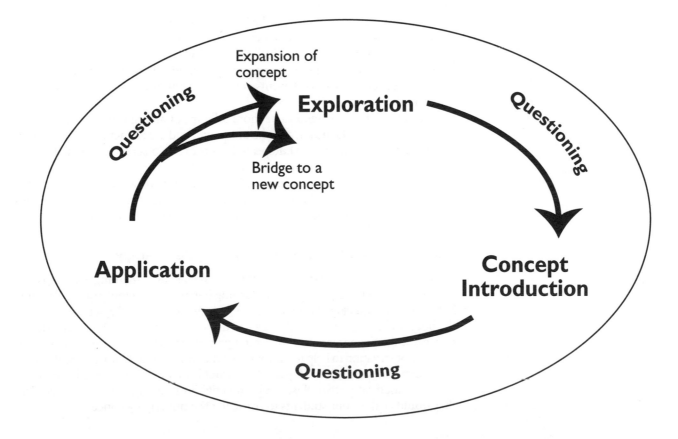

math). Often, application activities can also be used for evaluation purposes. An assessment of an application activity can be combined with student written work, student interviews, and your informal observations. Comparing a Learning Cycle approach to Piaget's model of learning, Renner and Marek (1988) suggest that exploration fosters assimilation and disequilibrium, concept introduction provides for accommodation, and application accomplishes organization.

Use of discrepant events in a Learning Cycle strategy

A powerful way to motivate your students is to use *discrepant events*. Discrepant events are encounters or phenomena that are puzzling to students and cannot be immediately assimilated to previous ways of thinking. The contradictions raised by the puzzling observations create a state of "disequilibrium" and stimulate students to attempt to resolve the contradiction (Berlyne 1965).

A certain amount of anxiety appears to be helpful in "luring" students to attempt to resolve the discrepancy (Frymier 1974). Bigge (1976) suggests that when student perplexity is just short of frustration, motivation is at its highest. However, we must be very careful that the problem raised by the discrepant event is not so difficult, ambiguous, or dissonant that the student is overwhelmed and unable to proceed (Frymier 1974).

Also, we must be sure that our students have been exposed to the specific prerequisite concepts, skills, and techniques that will allow them to perceive the new phenomenon as discrepant and will enable them to suggest hypotheses and procedures for collecting data that will resolve the discrepancy. For example, the observation that water *expands* when it freezes is discrepant to students only if they have been led to infer from previous activities that liquids expand when heated and contract when cooled. To know exactly when in the sequence of selected activities to introduce students to this unique property of water as a discrepant event, we must know when it will be truly discrepant for the greatest number of students in the class.

Discrepant events can provide the focus for both demonstrations and hands-on activities. They can be a problem focus in the exploration activities of a Learning Cycle and are particularly effective "grabbers" when a new topic is being introduced. They can also be used during the Application Phase to reinforce or to expand the concept. Discrepant events are a consistent motivation for the activities found in this book.

Motivated students tend to be more tolerant of ambiguity, are better able to assimilate the new, the novel, and the unknown, and are attracted to the unfamiliar or unclear (Frymier 1974). Repeated exposure to discrepant events followed by their successful resolution should help students develop an increased tolerance for ambiguity. Since students with a more positive self-concept tend to be better able to perceive and cope with greater dissonance (Frymier 1974), the importance of developing positive self-concepts in our students is clear.

How to develop and use a Learning Cycle strategy

Imagine that one of your students tells you that she saw something exciting on TV last night. Mr. Wizard put a piece of burning paper into an empty quart glass milk bottle and then quickly placed one end of a peeled hard boiled egg into the hole in the bottle; after a few seconds the egg was drawn into the bottle. She then asks you to explain the phenomenon. How would you use the motivation provided by this puzzling observation to help teach your class the concept that temperature affects the expansion and contraction of gases? How would you organize the egg-in-the-bottle demonstration and other closely related activities into an instructional sequence that would enable your students to construct the underlying concept?

After performing the demonstration with your class, resist the temptation to explain the phenomenon. Rather, let your students identify possible hypotheses to explain why the egg is being drawn into the bottle. This will help you identify any preconceptions and misconceptions your students may have related to the concept underlying the demonstration.

Next, present a sequence of related activities that will help your students resolve the problem raised by the egg-in-the-bottle phenomenon and construct an explanation (or concept) that will satisfactorily explain what was observed in all the activities. Once the concept has been introduced, you can identify additional activities that help students apply and reinforce the concept to new situations.

Developing and using Learning Cycles in your classroom involves a number of tasks that deviate significantly from those performed in more traditional science teaching. You can use the following sequence as a guide.

1. Choose a general topic from your textbook or curriculum guide, like heat.

2. Identify a discrete concept related to the topic, like convection. Selecting a more discrete focus for each Learning Cycle makes it easier to identify and sequence activities related to the particular concept. (In many textbook lessons on the topic of heat, for example, heat is discussed in terms of its movement through solids, liquids, and gases and, typically, three concepts are introduced— conduction, convection, and radiation. By developing Learning Cycles for each of the three discrete concepts, students can more easily identify similarities and differences among these concepts.)

3. Decide on overall goals and objectives for teaching the selected concept. Be sure to include objectives that develop student thinking skills and attitudes as well as more content-oriented objectives.

4. Select any examples or activities in your curriculum guide or student textbook that can be used as part of your Learning Cycle.

5. Identify other activities and examples of the concept from available sources. The *Appendix* provides a list of resource books containing hands-on activities and demonstrations for teachers. You need enough activities for the Exploration and Application Phases, and you may want to use additional activities to reinforce the concept throughout the year and to evaluate student understanding of the concept.

6. Identify objectives for each activity you select. Try to achieve as many objectives as possible with each activity. One way to achieve a greater variety of objectives is to make an activity less structured, more open-ended, thus providing more opportunities to develop science processes.

7. Rewrite each activity to conform as much as possible to a common format. (The format used for the activity sheets in this book is one of many; it is largely a matter of personal preference.) Think carefully about the questions you ask. Each question on the written activity sheet contains a science process. The question identifies the thinking skill used in the science process. Emphasizing the science processes will give your students a greater opportunity to demonstrate and apply these thinking skills in new situations both in science and in other subject areas.

8. Decide which activities will be performed by individual students, which will be performed within small groups, and which will be performed as teacher or student demonstrations. Time, availability of required materials and equipment, class size, student age, and classroom management concerns will affect these decisions.

9. Estimate the number of activities you will need in the exploration phase so a significant number of students can identify and communicate the characteristics of the concept. Select those activities that in your judgment best grab student attention and help develop the concept inductively.

10. From your remaining pool of activities, select those that can be used to reinforce, apply, and extend the concept within the application phase of your Learning Cycle.

11. Organize all of the activities into a logical sequence. The activities might progress from simple to more complex, or you might want to position motivational activities at strategic points within the Learning Cycle.

12. Make sure that any prerequisite concepts and skills needed by your students have been introduced and appropriately sequenced in the Learning Cycle.

13. Teach the concept. Be ready to move one or more of the activities from the Application Phase to the Exploration Phase if you see that your students have not yet reached the desired level of understanding. Also be ready to alter your sequence of activities as your students reveal their preconceptions and misconceptions. Your goal is to help a particular student or class arrive at the most accurate explanation of the phenomena observed.

14. Use additional examples and activities to evaluate your students either formally or informally.

15. Identify any children's trade books that can be used to reinforce or extend the concept topic.

When you feel ready to develop your *own* Learning Cycle sequence, examine the activities found in the Surface Tension Learning Cycle in Section III. This Learning Cycle contains activities and teacher background, but the activities are not sequenced. Develop a Learning Cycle sequence using all of the activities you feel you will need to enable students to construct an accurate concept regarding surface tension. Remember, your sequence will be a product of your own experiences, personality, and logic. Try it with your students and make any needed modifications based on student responses.

Integrating the science processes into a learning cycle

The science processes—observing, comparing and contrasting, ordering, categorizing, relating, and inferring, communicating, and applying (California State Board of Education 1990)—are integral to the Learning Cycle strategy. They are means through which students bring meaning to scientific concepts and relationships. You can help students think critically by using well-structured questions and questioning sequences that prompt the particular type or kind of science process students must use to obtain information about a particular concept. The science processes that are used in Section II are explained below.

Observing. Observing involves using the senses (sight, sound, taste, touch, and smell) to elicit the physical characteristics of an object, event, or situation. Observing is the primary way our students bring meaning to their experiences (Dantonio 1990).

Comparing and Contrasting. Comparing and Contrasting involve sorting information by identifying and distinguishing likenesses and differences. While comparing and contrasting are opposite skills, they are usually used simultaneously. Generally, comparing is the basis for concept formation. The commonalties found among phenomena, objects, and observations are the critical attributes of a concept. Contrasting, on the other hand, provides the foundation for discerning subconcepts and discovering the uniqueness among similar objects, situations, experiences.

Ordering.   Ordering is arranging content information by sequencing or seriating. In ordering, students arrange information in sequence along a continuum that establishes boundaries. Boundaries can be from most important to least important, from smallest to largest, from nearest to farthest.

Categorizing.   Categorizing involves assigning examples of a concept to preexisting or inductively determined categories. Two types of thinking are involved in categorizing: classifying examples into a known concept—identifying copper as a metal, for example—and grouping individual examples of a concept together by virtue of a common attribute, like placing a penny, a nail, and tinfoil together because each makes the light bulb glow when placed into a circuit. When students classify they identify the critical characteristics of new examples of an item or a concept and explain why the new example fits into a known category. Grouping involves collecting information about examples and determining the underlying concept. Grouping is more inductive than classifying, requiring students to discover a category rather than rely on a pre-established one (Dantonio 1990).

Relating.   Relating is identifying relationships—conditional, interactive, or cause and effect—between and among phenomena. Relationships are the blending of interactions, conditions, and cause and effect events operating together. Initially, in the Exploration Phase of a Learning Cycle sequence, hypothesizing is often used to assist students in brainstorming relationships. At this point in the Learning Cycle sequence, students often have neither the experience nor the mental structures to relate the phenomena they are being asked to explain. The use of relating questions can help identify student misconceptions. For example, what makes you say that the copper wire was the reason the bulb lit?

During the Application Phase, students are more likely to be able to state relationships between the concept that has been introduced earlier and a new phenomenon they have just observed. Predicting is often used in the Application Phase to help students see these relationships. Often, relating requires putting together complex and seemingly unrelated information gathered through studying how things intersect with the systems they have created, for example a battery, a bulb, and a bare copper wire are related because it takes the copper metal to conduct the current to light the bulb. It means that students must identify relationships that have meaning for them and can be validated through further manipulation of the data. The relating of information results in the creation of concepts which explain events, guide experimentation, and help students discriminate among variables.

There are three basic types of relationships: causal, effectual, and attribute. Causal relationships are reasons why concepts affect each other. In other words, students are answering the question, "What are the reasons why something happens?" Effectual relationships are the results of concepts that interact with each other. Students are determining, "What are the effects of using copper wires?" Attributes are the properties of specific concepts, attributes are what makes something what it is. For example, "What has to be true in order for a bulb to light?"

Hypothesizing and Predicting.   Hypothesizing and predicting are relationships which seek to explain phenomena. When a student states a hypothesis, the basis of the hypothesis may not be known because the student does not have the necessary information to explain his or her thinking; whereas, during predicting, the student should have formed a concept and have the background information that can be used to explain a phenomenon. For example, "What might raise the water in the bottle?" The word "might" indicates the student will be predicting or hypothesizing according to the phase of the Learning Cycle.

Inferring.   Inferring is constructing a well-reasoned conclusion from evidence. The conclusions are often based on relationships among information or data that extend from the known into the unknown. Inferring requires students to draw conclusions from the data and make educated guesses about objects, events, or situations in which all the facts are not present. They must support their assumptions, predictions, or conclusions by citing evidence. In constructing a sound argument for an inference, students go beyond the known information by logically presenting premises and factual evidence, and tie their premises to the evidence gathered.

Communicating.   Communicating is conveying understanding by writing papers, drawing diagrams, defining terms, making presentations, charting graphs, conducting demonstrations, or using other forms of illustration.

Applying.   Applying means extending newly acquired observations, ideas, or concepts to new situations. The application of information can be practical or theoretical.

EFFECTIVE QUESTIONING

You need to be aware of the phrasing and function of the questions you ask in order to elicit these science processes successfully. The questions you use in a Learning Cycle can guide, direct, focus, and facilitate student thinking. They can also provide opportunities for students to share their thinking with one another (Dantonio l990). You must know how to phrase, sequence, and pace your questions to help students shape quality responses and help them understand how they arrived at their answers. A Learning Cycle is planned and conducted through *core questions* and *processing questions.*

Phrasing core questions

The initial or core question cannot be sloppily phrased. First, the core question must be clear. It needs to accurately convey the thinking processes and content students will use in working through their investigations. Second, your core question must be open. An open question contains a word cue that stimulates the detailing of information. Beginning a question with *what, who, where, why, how,* or *in what way* ensures that students will respond with a statement rather than answer the question with *yes* or *no.* This type of question stimulates multiple responses from a number of students. Third, a core question must focus for the student on the science process to be used (Dantonio 1990).

The noun phrases used in core questions provide clues to the science content. The verb phrases of the questions trigger the specific science process. In the examples below the verb phrases that cue the *science process* **are shown in bold-face type.** The *openness* of the question is found in the first words of each example, which are *italicized.*

Observing: *What* **do you notice is happening** to the solution in the vial?

Comparing: *In what way* is what happens to the ball in the funnel experiment **like what happens when** we blow down on paper?

Ordering: *Arrange* **the solutions** in order from the one that contains the most acid to the one that contains the least acid.

Categorizing: *In what way* **can we group** the items on this table for density?

Relating: *What* **do you think causes** the match to go out when it is dropped in the bottle?

Inferring: *On what* **basis do you think** that example C **will light?**

Types of processing questions

A series of questions following a student response to the initial core question enables students to bring meaning to the content they acquire. These follow-up questions, referred to as processing questions, encourage the students to develop mental structures related to the content and topic. They also personalize the topic and the students' knowledge of the topic. Additionally, they give students the opportunity to share their observations and questions with one another, developing more accurate and elaborate content structures.

Processing questions are probes you use to help students rethink their answers and refine their understanding. Processing questions encourage students to clarify, extend, personalize, verify, and support their initial response (Dantonio l990). They also help you identify any student misconceptions about the topic. There are five types of processing questions: refocusing, clarifying, verifying, supporting, and redirecting.

1. *Refocusing questions* are used when students are not doing the thinking called for by the core question or when they are talking off the subject. An example of a refocusing question is, "You stated a difference between the two. I asked you to compare electricity and magnetism. What similarities do you find between the properties of electricity and magnetism?"

2. *Clarifying questions* help students understand science vocabulary and ideas; they also help students sharpen their ideas. You cannot assume that because students use a particular word or phrase that they understand what it means. A simple rule for facilitating student answers is: No matter how simple the concept or example, clarify! The more ways students define something, the more extensive their understanding will be. Clarifying questions ask students to define terminology or to define something operationally. Examples of clarifying questions are, "What do you mean by magnetism?" and "How do you define electricity?"

3. *Verifying questions* help students determine the accuracy of their responses. Verifying questions ask students to cite examples, share previously learned knowledge, cite authorities, or make generalizations that can be applied to the focus of the lesson. Verifying questions may also contribute to personalizing science concepts by encouraging students to state personal experiences or to share situations similar to the one being examined. More specifically, verifying questions require that students cite evidence for ideas. This is most important when they are relating and inferring. Typical examples of verifying questions are, "How do you know the copper wire is the conductor?" "Where have you experienced this before?" and "Give me an example of something that doesn't conduct electricity."

4. *Supporting questions* help students establish relationships between information, ideas, and concepts. They are especially important when students are categorizing, relating, and inferring. In each of these science processes, students must hook up or link information pertaining to a number of ideas. To help students understand how they constructed or pulled together their ideas, you can ask questions like, "What is there about the way the paper moved that leads you to say that there was a change in pressure around the paper?" and "On what basis do you make the statement, When air is cooled, it contracts?"

5. You use *redirecting questions* when you want either more than one response to any type of question or more student participation. Redirecting questions can help you pace the lesson because they allow you to wait for additional responses before moving on to another question or to additional content. Redirecting questions are a way to help your students deepen and widen their understanding through peer interaction. Examples of redirecting questions

are, "What other ways can we use this information?" "Who else notices something about the flame?" and "Give me some other examples of things that conduct electricity."

Question sequencing

Careful attention to core and processing questions can help teachers create *questioning sequences*. These encourage interactive patterns in the classroom that are conducive to teaching and learning. To prepare Learning Cycles that trigger the science processes through effective questions and questioning sequences, ask yourself the following planning questions:

1. Which science process(es) do I want students to use to obtain information?
2. How do I phrase core question(s) to elicit the needed information?
3. What types of responses could students provide for the core question(s)?
4. What processing questions are needed to refocus, extend, or strengthen the responses students give to the core question?

The answers to these questions provide a blueprint for conducting lessons within each phase of the Learning Cycle. If you are going to ask effective core questions and know which processing questions to ask when, you must listen carefully to what your students are saying. The more you practice using the questions and questioning sequences to initiate the science processes, the more adept you will become at facilitating student thinking and classroom interactions.

Figure 2 is a generic summary of suggestions for combining science process core questions and follow-up processing questions.

SCIENCE CORE QUESTIONS		PROCESSING QUESTIONS	
Core Process	**Question Stem**	**Question Type**	**Question Stem**
OBSERVING	What do you notice about ____?	CLARIFYING	What do you mean by___?
COMPARING	How are these alike?	VERIFYING	How do you know? or Give me an example
CONTRASTING	How are these different?	SUPPORTING	What makes you say ____ about ____?
ORDERING	How can we arrange_____?	REDIRECTING	What other ____? or Who else___?
CATEGORIZING	Which of these go together? or Which of these are examples of ____?	REFOCUSING	You said ____. I asked you to ___, so reask the question.
RELATING	What are the causes for___? or What are the effects of____?		
HYPOTHESIZING AND PREDICTING	What do you predict about __? or What attributes can you assign to ___? or What do you think will happen if___? or What will be the results of___?		
INFERRING	What do you infer/ about ____? or On what basis do you think ___?		
COMMUNICATING	How can we show this?		
APPLYING	How can we apply this?		

Summary of Science Core Questions and Processsing Questions

There is increasing evidence that science concepts developed by students experiencing a Learning Cycle approach are more scientifically accurate and less dependent on the students' own preconceptions (Marek, Cowan, and Cavallo 1994), but the goal of using a Learning Cycle strategy is not just to help your students develop and extend science concepts. It is also to help them understand how science content is generated and tested. Through your expert use of questions and question sequences, students will start learning how to become skillful scientific thinkers.

REFERENCES

American Association for the Advancement of Science. 1989. *Project 2061: Science for All Americans.* Washington, D.C.: American Association for the Advancement of Science.

Barman, C.R., and Kotar, M. 1989. "The Learning Cycle." *Science and Children* 26 (7): 30–32.

Barman, C.R., and Shedd, J.D. 1992. "An Inservice Program Designed to Introduce K–6 Teachers to a Learning Cycle Approach." *Journal of Science Teacher Education* 3 (2): 58–64.

Barnes, M.B., Shaw, T.J., and Spector, B.S. 1989. *How Science Is Learned by Adolescents and Young Adults.* Dubuque, IA: Kendall Hunt Publishing Co.

Beisenherz, P.C. 1991. "Explore, invent, and apply." *Science and Children* 28 (4): 30–32.

Berlyne, D.E. 1965. "Curiosity and education." In *Learning and the Educational Process,* ed. J.D. Krumbultz. Chicago: Rand McNally and Company.

Bigge, M. 1976. *Learning Theories for Teachers.* New York: Harper and Row.

Brooks, J.G., and Brooks, M.G. 1993. *In Search of Understanding: The Case for Constructivist Classrooms.* Alexandria, Virginia: Association for Supervision and Curriculum Development (ASCD).

Dantonio, M. l990. *How Can We Create Thinkers? Questioning Strategies That Work for Teachers.* Bloomington, IN: National Education Services.

Fleury, S.C., and Bentley, M.L. 1991. "Educating Elementary Science Teachers: Alternative Conceptions of the Nature of Science." *Teaching Education* 3 (2): 57–67.

Frymier, J.R. 1974. *Motivation and Learning in School: Fastback 43.* Bloomington, IN: Phi Delta Kappa.

Glasson, G.E., and Lalik, R.V. 1993. "Reinterpreting the Learning Cycle from a Social Constructivist Perspective: A Qualitative Study of Teachers' Beliefs and Practices." *Journal of Research in Science Teaching* 30 (2): 187–207.

Haney, R.E. 1964. "The Development of Scientific Attitudes." *The Science Teacher* 31 (8): 33–35.

Jacobson, W., and Kondo, A. 1968. "Science Curriculum Improvement Study." In *SCIS Elementary Science Sourcebook.* Berkeley, California: University of California.

Karplus, R., and Thier, H.D. 1967. *A New Look at Elementary School Science.* Chicago: Rand McNally.

Lawson, A.E. 1988. "A Better Way to Teach Biology." *The American Biology Teacher* 50 (5): 266–274.

Lawson, A.E., Abramham, M.R., and Renner, J.W. 1989. *A Theory of Instruction: Using the Learning Cycle to Teach Science Concepts and Thinking Skills.* Columbus, Oh: National Association for Research in Science Teaching (NARST), Monograph Number One.

Marek, E.A., Cowan, C.C., and Cavallo, A.M.L. 1994 "Students' Misconceptions about Diffusion: How Can They Be Eliminated?" *The American Biology Teacher* 56 (2):74–77.

Mechling, K.R., and Oliver, D.L. 1983. *What Research Says About Elementary School Science* (Handbook IV). Washington, D.C.:National Science Teachers Association.

Pearsall, M.K., ed. 1992. *Scope, Sequence, and Coordination of Secondary School Science,* Volume II: *Relevant Research.*Washington, D.C.: The National Science Teachers Association.

Penick, J.E., ed. 1983. *Focus on Excellence: Elementary Science.* Washington, D.C.: National Science Teachers Association.

Pratt, H. 1981. "Science Education in the Elementary School." In *What Research Says to the Science Teacher,* Volume 3, Harms, N.C., and Yager, R.E., eds. Washington, D.C.: National Science Teachers Association.

Renner, J.W., and Marek, E.A. 1988. *The Learning Cycle and Elementary School Science Teaching.* Portsmouth, NH: Heinemann.

———. 1990. "An Educational Theory Base for Science Teaching." *Journal of Research in Science Teaching* 27 (3): 241–246.

Rubba, P.A., and Klindienst, D.B., eds. 1990. *Teacher Developed Elementary Science — Learning Cycle Lesson Plans.* Pennsylvania State University. NSF Grant No. TEI–8651678 and Pennsylvania Department of Education Grant No. HO–61104-C, 20–6822. University Park, PA: Pennsylvania State University.

Science: A Process. Approach II (SAPA II) 1974. Nashua, Delta Education, Inc.

Science Framework for California Public Schools. 1990. Sacramento, CA: California Department of Education.

Shymansky, J.A., Kyle, W.C., Jr., and Alport, J.M. 1982. "How Effective were the Hands-on Science Programs of Yesterday?" *Science and Children* 20 (3): 14–15.

Shymansky, J.A. 1992. "Using Constructivist Ideas to Teach Science Teachers about Constructivist Ideas, or Teachers are Students Too!" *Journal of Science Teacher Education* 3 (2): 53–57.

Tobin, K., ed. 1993. *The Practice of Constructivism in Science Education.* Washington, D.C.: American Association for the Advancement of Science Press.

Von Glaserfeld, E. 1989. "Cognition, Construction of Knowledge, and Teaching." *Synthese* 80, 121–140.

Watson, B., and Konicek, R. 1990. "Teaching for Conceptual Change: Confronting Children's Experience. *Phi Delta Kappan* 71 (9): 680–685.

Wheatley, G.H. 1991. "Constructivist Perspectives on Science and Mathematics Learning." *Science Education* 75 (1):9–21.

Yager, R.E. 1991. "The Constructivist Learning Model." *The Science Teacher* 58 (6): 52–57.

SIX LEARNING CYCLES

Bernoulli's Principle

▼

CONCEPT: *The pressure inside a region of air is lower when the air is moving than when the air is standing still (Bernoulli's Principle).*

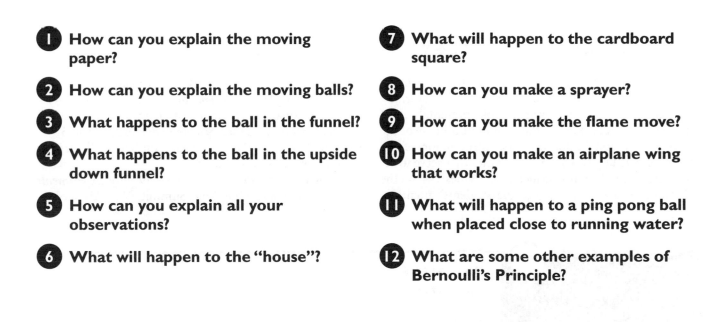

1 How can you explain the moving paper?

2 How can you explain the moving balls?

3 What happens to the ball in the funnel?

4 What happens to the ball in the upside down funnel?

5 How can you explain all your observations?

6 What will happen to the "house"?

7 What will happen to the cardboard square?

8 How can you make a sprayer?

9 How can you make the flame move?

10 How can you make an airplane wing that works?

11 What will happen to a ping pong ball when placed close to running water?

12 What are some other examples of Bernoulli's Principle?

SUGGESTED LEARNING CYCLE SEQUENCE

Exploration Activities: Activities 1 to 4

Concept Introduction: Activity 5

Application Activities: Activities 6 to 12

INTRODUCTION

The faster a fluid stream (such as air or water) moves, the lower is the pressure associated with the stream. Pressure is a result of random molecular collisions upon a surface. However, if the molecular collisions upon a surface are no longer random, there can be a change in pressure. For example, in Activity 2, the molecules of air were moving randomly around the two tennis balls. By blowing a stream of air between the two balls, however, many of the air molecules that were moving randomly between the two balls are now in a stream moving in one direction between the balls. As a result, the *lower* pressure produced in this stream, as compared to the surrounding air, causes the movement of the balls into the stream of moving air.

Upon completing this Learning Cycle, students should be able to identify four attributes or characteristics common to all activities they have observed: (1) moving air; (2) air moving in one direction; (3) differences in pressure between upper and lower and inner and outer surfaces that cause an object (tennis ball, ping pong ball, sheet of paper) to move in the direction of the moving stream (region of lower pressure); and (4) the faster the moving stream, the lower the pressure and the greater the movement of an object in the direction of the lower pressure.

The introduction of the concept of Bernoulli's Principle (Concept Introduction Phase) occurs in Activity 5. Activities 6–12 make up the Application Phase. Some of the activities in this third phase could be used as home activities or learning center experiences for students. The activities have been written as instructions and questions for your students, and each is accompanied by background information for you. As you work with students on the activities, feel free to make use of the drawings and charts included here. You may want to recreate some of the charts on an overhead transparency or on the blackboard so your students can refer to them.

As in the teaching of any concept using a Learning Cycle strategy, there is no correct number and sequence of examples. Many factors—including the difficulty of the concept, age and background of the students, teacher background, interests, and logic—help you determine how a concept is presented to students. The sequence identified in this Learning Cycle sequence generally proceeds from simpler to more difficult examples. Using a Learning Cycle approach, your role is to supplement these basic activities with others gleaned from a variety of sources. These new activities are then added to the existing text activities and then placed into a Learning Cycle sequence.

LEARNING CYCLE STRATEGY

These activities are organized around the concept of Bernoulli's Principle and represent one possible Learning Cycle sequence. Typically, a textbook presentation of Bernoulli's Principle excludes the Exploration Phase of the Learning Cycle and begins with the introduction of the concept followed by two or three activities that serve to reinforce the concept. In this sequence, Activities 1–4 are the Exploration Phase. They engage the students' attention.

REFERENCES

Barnes, G.B. 1984. "Curve Balls, Airplane Wings, and Prairie Dog Holes." *Science and Children* 21 (8): 13–15.

Keller, E.L. 1986. "Fore, Batter Up, Love 15—A Lesson in Bernoulli's Principle." *Science Activities* 23 (4): 4–5.

Kesling, M.D. 1987. "Up in the Air with Bernoulli." *Science and Children* 24 (4): 26–27.

Wood, R.W. 1989. *Physics for Kids—49 Easy Experiments with Mechanics.* Blue Ridge Summit, PA.: TAB Books.

ACTIVITY 1

How Can You Explain the Moving Paper?

MATERIALS

one sheet of paper

WHAT TO DO

▼ Hold a sheet of paper at mouth level as in the picture below.
▼ Hold the paper with both hands between the thumb and index finger.

HYPOTHESIZING	**What do you think will happen when you blow hard across the top surface of the sheet of paper?**
APPLYING	*Try it!*
OBSERVING	**What did you observe?**
SUPPORTING	**What reasons can you give for your observations?**

TEACHER BACKGROUND INFORMATION

Prior to blowing across the top surface of the paper the molecules of air were moving randomly on both sides of the paper resulting in equal pressure on both sides. However, by blowing across the top surface of the paper, many of those molecules above the top surface that were moving randomly are now in a stream moving in one direction. As a result, the air pressure above the surface is lowered as there are fewer molecules moving downward to strike the paper. The pressure in the fast-moving stream of air flowing above the sheet of paper is lower than the pressure in the still air underneath the paper. The higher pressure of the air underneath compared to the lower pressure above makes the paper rise. Students should observe that the harder they blow (the faster the moving stream of air), the higher the paper will rise in the air.

ACTIVITY 2

How Can You Explain the Moving Balls?

MATERIALS

two tennis balls   ping pong balls or balloons
strings   masking tape

WHAT TO DO

▼ Use masking tape to attach one end of a string to a tennis ball.
▼ Repeat with another string and ball.
▼ Hang the balls from a horizontal bar.
▼ The two strings should be about 12–16 inches long.
▼ The two balls should be placed about one inch apart.
▼ Put your mouth within 2–3 inches of the balls.

HYPOTHESIZING   **What do you think will happen to the balls when you blow a steady stream of air between them?**

APPLYING   *Try it!*

OBSERVING   **What did you observe?**

SUPPORTING   **What reasons can you give for your observations?**

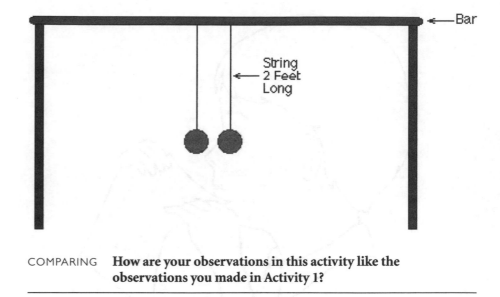

COMPARING   **How are your observations in this activity like the observations you made in Activity 1?**

TEACHER BACKGROUND INFORMATION

Prior to blowing between the two tennis balls, the molecules of air were moving randomly around the two balls. However, by blowing between the two balls, many of those molecules that were moving randomly between the two balls are now in a stream moving in one direction between the balls. As a result, the air pressure between the balls is lowered as there are fewer molecules hitting the inside surface of the two balls. The pressure in the fast-moving airstream blown between the balls is less than the pressure exerted by the still air surrounding the balls. The randomly moving molecules in the still air push the balls together. Students should observe that the harder they blow (the faster the moving stream of air), the greater the movement of the balls towards each other. Ping pong balls or balloons are good substitutes for the tennis balls.

ACTIVITY **3**

What Happens to the Ball in the Funnel?

MATERIALS

funnel with a stem   ping pong ball
rubbing alcohol   paper towel

WHAT TO DO

▼ Clean the stem end of the funnel by dipping it into a small cup of alcohol.
▼ Wipe the stem dry with a paper towel.
▼ Put the ping pong ball inside the funnel.
▼ Hold the funnel upright as in the picture below while standing.

HYPOTHESIZING   **What do you think will happen to the ball when you blow as hard as you can through the narrow opening of the funnel?**

▼ Place your lips on the tip of the stem and blow as hard as you can.

OBSERVING   **What did you notice happened to the ball?**
SUPPORTING   **What reasons can you give for your observations?**
COMPARING   **How are your observations in this activity like your observations in Activities 1 and 2?**

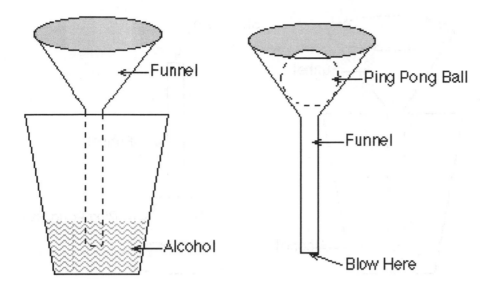

TEACHER BACKGROUND INFORMATION

The ping pong ball does not blow out of the funnel but spins close to the sides. Blowing air through the funnel results in rapidly moving air going in one direction around the inside of the funnel next to the ping pong ball. The air pressure in this stream of moving air is less than the air above the funnel. As a result, the ping pong ball moves into the stream of moving air causing it to remain in the funnel.

<table>
<tr><td>ACTIVITY 4</td></tr>
<tr><td>What Happens to the Ball in the Upside Down Funnel?</td></tr>
</table>

MATERIALS

funnel with a stem   ping pong ball
rubbing alcohol   paper towel

WHAT TO DO

▼ Clean the stem end of the funnel by dipping it into a small cup of rubbing alcohol. Wipe the stem dry with a paper towel. Put a ping pong ball inside the funnel. Hold your hand over the top of the funnel and turn the funnel upside down.

HYPOTHESIZING   **What do you think will happen to the ball when you blow as hard as you can through the narrow opening of the funnel?**

▼ While blowing through the funnel, remove your hand from the bottom of the funnel.

OBSERVING   **What did you notice happened to the ball?**
APPLYING   **Using your funnel, try picking up the ping pong ball withoug using your hands**
COMMUNICATING   **Describe how you were able to do it.**
OBSERVING   **What did you observe?**
SUPPORTING   **What reasons can you give for your observations?**
COMPARING   **How are your observations in this activity like your observations in Activities 1, 2, and 3?**

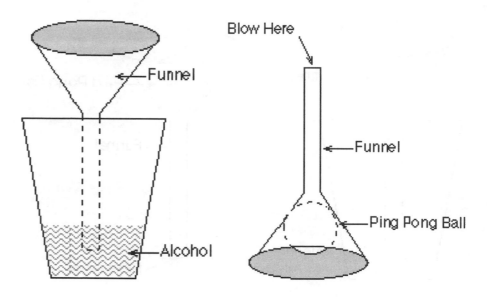

TEACHER BACKGROUND INFORMATION

When the funnel is inverted, the ball should not fall out as long as a strong stream of air is blown through the stem. Prior to class, try using your breath to keep the ball inside the inverted funnel. If you cannot keep the ball inside the funnel, locate a resource person—like another teacher, the principal, or the custodian—who can. Students should be able to pick up the ball that is resting on the table by laying the open end of the funnel over the ball and blowing very hard through the stem of the funnel.

ACTIVITY 5

How Can You Explain All Your Observations?

COMPARING	**How are your observations in activities 1, 2, 3, and 4 alike?**
CONTRASTING	**How are they different?**
INFERRING	**What conclusion can you make from all your observations in activities 1, 2, 3, and 4?**

TEACHER BACKGROUND INFORMATION

Ask students what activities 1–4 have in common. Students should be able to infer that activities 1–4 have four attributes or characteristics in common: (1) moving air; (2) air moving in one direction; (3) differences in pressure between upper and lower and inner and outer surfaces that cause an object (tennis ball, ping pong ball, sheet of paper) to move in the direction of the moving stream (region of lower pressure); and (4) the faster the moving stream, the lower the pressure and the greater the movement of an object in the direction of the lower pressure. If students are unable to communicate these relationships, be ready to move one or more activities you have designated for the Application Phase to the Exploration Phase. Through your questions you can determine if your students see the relationships among the various activities.

ACTIVITY 6

What Will Happen to the "House"?

MATERIALS

one 8 ½ × 11-inch piece of paper

WHAT TO DO

▼ Fold a piece of paper to make a "house" and set the "house" on a table.

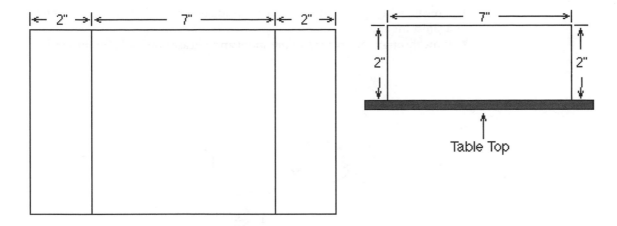

Table Top

PREDICTING	**What do you predict will happen when you blow hard under the "house"?**
APPLYING	*Try it!*
OBSERVING	**What did you observe?**
INFERRING	**What conclusion can you draw from your observation?**

TEACHER BACKGROUND INFORMATION

Students should predict and observe that blowing a stream of air through the "house" creates a region of lower pressure causing the "house" to collapse.

ACTIVITY **7**

What Will Happen to the Cardboard Square?

MATERIALS:

one 3 × 5-inch card cut into a square (3 × 3 inches)
spool of thread (with or without the thread)

straight pin   ruler

WHAT TO DO

▼ On your cardboard square draw diagonal lines from each corner (see the picture below).
▼ Stick a straight pin through the card where the lines cross at the center.
▼ Place the pin into the hole in a spool of thread.

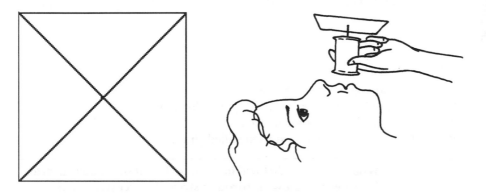

PREDICTING	**What do you think will happen to the cardboard square when you lie on your back and blow through the hole?**
APPLYING	*Try it!*
OBSERVING	**What did you observe happening to the square when you blew?**

▼ Now turn the spool, pin, and square upside down and hold the card lightly against the spool.
▼ Blow through the opening in the spool and release your hold on the card.

OBSERVING	**What did you notice happening to the square when you blew this time?**
INFERRING	**What conclusion can you make from your observation?**
COMPARING	**How are your observations in this activity like the observations you made in the earlier activities?**

TEACHER BACKGROUND INFORMATION

Students should predict and observe that when air is blown through the spool the card will not blow off the spool or fall off the spool when the spool is inverted. They should infer that the pressure in the fast-moving stream of air between the card and the spool is lower than the pressure in the still air on the other side of the card.

ACTIVITY (8)

How Can You Make a Sprayer?

MATERIALS

soda straw cut in half   cup
colored water

WHAT TO DO

Set up the materials as shown below.
▼ Place half of a soda straw (A) in a cup of colored water.
▼ Fill the straw (A) with colored water.
▼ Hold an empty straw (B) next to the filled straw.

PREDICTING	**What do you predict will happen to the colored water in straw (A) when you blow air through straw (B) over straw (A)?**
APPLYING	*Try it!*
OBSERVING	**What did you observe?**
INFERRING	**What conclusion can you make from your observation?**
COMPARING	**How are your observations in this activity like the observations you made in earlier activities?**

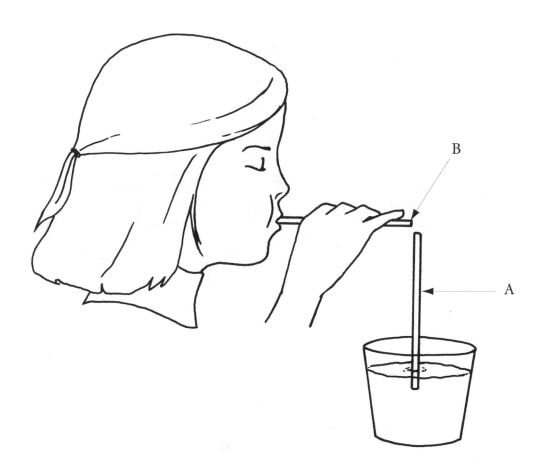

TEACHER BACKGROUND INFORMATION

Students should predict and observe that the colored water in the straw will rise to the top of the vertical straw and spray out. They should infer that blowing a stream of air rapidly across the top of the straw lowers the air pressure both inside the horizontal straw and in the region right above the vertical straw. The higher-pressure air in the "still" air next to the surface of the water in the glass pushes the water up the straw. This activity provides a rough model for how many atomizers and insect and paint spray guns operate.

ACTIVITY **9**

**How Will the Candle
Flame Move?**

MATERIALS

3 × 5-inch card cut into a 3 × 3-inch square

1 funnel with stem   1 candle
matches

WHAT TO DO

▼ Hold a 3-inch square piece of cardboard in front of a lighted candle.

PREDICTING	**What do you predict will happen to the flame of the candle when you blow hard toward the cardboard?**
APPLYING	*Try it!*
OBSERVING	**What did you observe?**
INFERRING	**What conclusion can you make from your observation?**

PREDICTING	**What do you predict will happen to the flame when you blow at it through the stem of the funnel?**
APPLYING	***Try it!***
OBSERVING	**What did you observe?**
INFERRING	**What conclusion can you make from your observation?**
COMPARING	**How are your observations in this activity like the observations you made in earlier activities?**

TEACHER BACKGROUND INFORMATION

When air is blown hard toward the cardboard, students should predict and observe the flame moving *toward* them. The flame will move toward the students because the airstream is directed over, under, and around the card, producing a low-pressure area behind the card. The higher-pressure air in the "still" air next to the flame "pushes" the flame toward the card. Likewise, students should predict that the flame will bend toward the funnel. They should infer that the pressure is lower in the moving airstream than in the surrounding air. The higher-pressure air in the "still" air moves toward the lower-pressure area and "pushes" the flame toward the funnel.

MATERIALS

soda straw   3 × 5-inch card
ruler   6-sided pencil

WHAT TO DO

RELATING   **How does the shape of the wing help make an airplane fly?**

To help you answer this question, make the airplane wing as described below.
▼ Tape a card to one end of a ruler.
▼ Make the card curve up like the top of an airplane wing.
▼ Balance the ruler across a six-sided pencil.
▼ The ruler should very lightly tip down at the card end.
▼ Blow air through the soda straw across the curved top of the card.

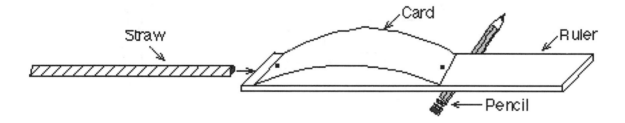

PREDICTING   **What will happen to the ruler when you blow air through the straw?**
APPLYING   ***Try it!***
OBSERVING   **What did you observe?**
INFERRING   **What conclusion can you make from your observation?**
CONTRASTING   **During flight, how is the air flowing above the wing different from air flowing below the wing?**
RELATING   **How does this difference help the plane fly?**
COMPARING   **How are your observations in this activity like the observations you made in earlier activities?**

TEACHER BACKGROUND INFORMATION

Students should predict and observe that the low end of the ruler will rise. Students need to be patient in finding the ruler's point of balance. Have students try the activity without the card. Although the ruler without the card should rise, the curved surface of the card should enable the ruler to rise more easily.

The shape of the wing causes air to move faster over the top of the wing and more slowly underneath the wing. The difference between the higher pressure on the bottom and the lower pressure on the top of the wing helps to make the plane rise.

ACTIVITY 11

What Will Happen to a Ping Pong Ball When Placed Close to Running Water?

MATERIALS

ping pong ball
water faucet

12-inch string or thread
tape

WHAT TO DO

▼ Use a small piece of masking tape to attach the end of a piece of string or thread to a ping pong ball.

▼ Turn on the water faucet so that there is a steady stream of water.

▼ Hold the string so that the ping pong ball is about 6 inches from the water stream. (See the picture below.)

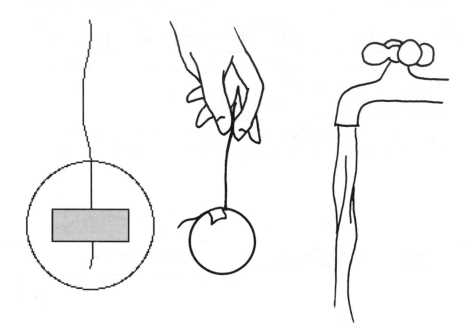

PREDICTING	**What do you think will happen to the ping pong ball when you move it *slowly* to about 1 inch away from the water stream?**
APPLYING	***Try it!***
OBSERVING	**What did you observe?**
PREDICTING	**What will happen when the ball touches the water stream?**
APPLYING	***Try it!***
INFERRING	**What conclusion can you make from your observations?**

▼ Again, hold the string so that the ping pong ball is about 6 inches from the water stream. Now open the faucet more fully so that the water pressure is increased.

PREDICTING	**What do you predict will happen to the ping pong ball as you move it closer to the stream of water?**
APPLYING	***Try it!***
OBSERVING	**What did you observe?**
RELATING	**What reason can you offer to explain any differences you observed in the movement of the ping pong ball that might be due to changes in the water pressure?**
CONTRASTING	**How is this activity different from other activities you have done related to Bernoulli's Principle?**

COMPARING **How is this activity like other activities you have done related to Bernoullli's Principle?**

INFERRING **Based on your experiences with activities demonstrating Bernoulli's Principle, what are the main points to remember about the principle?**

TEACHER BACKGROUND INFORMATION

Students should predict and observe that the ping pong ball will move toward and "adhere" to the stream of water because of the reduced pressure of the air created by the rapid motion of the fluid (water). Note that this is the only activity in the sequence that uses a fluid (water) instead of air.

ACTIVITY 12

What Are Some Other Examples of Bernoulli's Principle?

Here are some additional examples of Bernoulli's Principle:

1. Throwing a boomerang
2. Sailing a sailboat
3. Throwing a curve ball
4. Producing an updraft in a chimney
5. Moving of shower curtain toward the stream of water from shower
6. Moving of curtain out of an open window on a windy day
7. Moving of cigarette smoke out of a slightly opened window of a moving automobile

CATEGORIZING **Using the concept you have learned, how can you explain each of the above examples?**

CATEGORIZING **What other examples of Bernoulli's Principle can you identify?**

Acids and Bases

▼

CONCEPT: *an acid is any substance that turns a blue BTB solution Yellow; a base is any substance that turns a yellow BTB solution blue; and a neutral substance is any substance that does not change the color of a blue or yellow BTB solution.*

1 How can you make the blue solution change colors?

2 Which substances change the color of BTB?

3 How can you change the color of litmus paper?

4 How can you make your own indicators?

5 Which liquid contains the most acid?

6 How can you determine the strength of an acid using pH paper?

7 What is the best tablet to take for an upset stomach?

8 How will an Alka-Seltzer tablet affect the color of BTB?

SUGGESTED LEARNING CYCLE SEQUENCE

Exploration Activities: Activities 1 to 2

Concept Introduction: Activity 2

Application Activities: Activities 3 to 8

INTRODUCTION

Different solutions have many different properties. One way that solutions can be classified is whether they are *acidic, basic,* or *neutral*. In this Learning Cycle sequence, solutions are tested using several different indicators. The initial indicator used is bromothymol blue (BTB). It is easily obtained in the aquarium section of most pet shops or at various supply houses. A vial of BTB powder can be obtained from many supply houses. Because only a pinch is needed to make a quart or more of the blue solution, a vial of powder will last many years. When a drop or two of vinegar (an acid) is added to a blue solution of BTB, the color changes to yellow, indicating the presence of an acid. When a basic solution, such as liquid ammonia or baking soda, is added to the blue BTB solution, no change occurs. However, a blue color will result when the ammonia or baking soda solution is added to a *yellow* BTB solution. No color change is observed when a "neutral" solution such as sugar water is added to either a blue or yellow BTB solution. In testing a number of solutions in Activities 1 and 2, students observe color changes, group or classify their observations, identify similarities and differences, and draw inferences to explain their observations.

At the end of Activity 2, students should be able to operationally define an acid as any substance that turns a blue BTB solution yellow, a base as any substance that turns a yellow BTB solution blue, and a neutral substance as any substance that does not change the color of a blue or yellow BTB solution.

LEARNING CYCLE STRATEGY

In this sequence, Activities 1 and 2 form the Exploration Phase of the Learning Cycle. The introduction of the concepts of acid/base/neutral substances occurs at the end of Activity 2 (Concept Introduction). The remaining activities serve to extend and reinforce the concepts (Application Phase). The activities have been written as instructions and questions for your students and each is accompanied by background information for you. As you work with students on the activities, feel free to make use of the drawings and charts included here. You may want to recreate some of the charts on an overhead transparency or on the blackboard so your students can refer to them.

SAFETY

Although the materials used in this sequence are relatively safe, students should be reminded *not* to taste any liquids without your permission. All solutions used in this Learning Cycle can be disposed of safely down the sink. Following Activity 5, it should be stressed to students that all acids and bases should be carefully handled. They should also be reminded that some acids and some bases are quite strong and dangerous. If students are encouraged to find other examples of acids and bases at home or around their school, be sure to communicate to students (and parents) any specific chemicals that may be hazardous, including bleach, Saniflush, Draino, and Muriatic Acid. While the acids and bases used in this sequence are not considered strong, it is desirable that your students become comfortable with using safety goggles. Their use is recommended.

MATERIALS

The following materials needed in the teaching of this Learning Cycle can be purchased from science supply companies such as Delta Education, P. O. Box M, Nashua, NH. 03601–6012 (1–800–258–1302): bromothymol blue, medicine droppers, medicine cups, clear plastic vials with lids, mortar and pestle, dropper (squeeze) bottles, safety goggles, 25 ml graduated cylinder.

REFERENCES

Acid Rain: Teacher's Guide. 1990. Great Explorations in Math & Science (GEMS). Berkeley, CA: Lawrence Hall of Science, University of California.

"Antacids—Which Beat Heartburn Best?" 1994. *Consumer Reports* 59 (7): 443–447.

Balloons and Gases: Teacher's Guide. 1985. Elementary Science Studies Series. Nashua, NH: Delta Education.

Beisenherz, P.C. 1981. "Fizz-fizz Science." *Science and Children* 19 (1): 30–32.

Domel, R. l993. "You Can Teach about Acid Rain." *Science and Children* 31 (2): 25–28.

Hanif, M. 1984. "Acid rain." *Science and Children* 22 (3): 19–22.

Hanshumaker, W. 1987. "A Head for Chemistry." *Science and Children* 25 (3): 24–26.

Kitchen Interactions: Teacher's Guide. 1981. SAVI/SELPH, Berkeley, CA: Center for Multisensory Learning, Lawrence Hall of Science.

Klein, J.S. 1976. "Red Cabbage Juice: It's Indicative!" *Science and Children* 13 (5): 17–18.

Marson, R. 1991. *Analysis: A Task Card Module: Teacher's Guide.* Task Oriented Physical Science (TOPS). Canby, OR: TOPS Learning Systems.

Of Cabbages and Chemistry: Teacher's Guide. 1989. Great Explorations Math & Science (GEMS). Berkeley, CA: Lawrence Hall of Science, University of California.

Phillips, D.B. 1986. "The Magic Sign: Acids, Bases, and Indicators. *Science and Children* 23 (4): 121–123.

Sae, A. 1990. "Of Cabbages and . . . Anthocyanins," *The Science Teacher* 57 (7): 16–18.

Sullivan, A. 1989. "Acid basics." *Science and Children* 27 (2): 22–24.

Three Gases. 1975. Science: A Process Approach II (Module 92). Nashua, NH: Delta Education, Inc.

MATERIALS

one pint (500 ml) blue bromothymol blue solution (BTB)
(2 medicine droppers could substitute for the squeeze bottles)
2-ounce squeeze bottle of nonsudsy clear ammonia
2-ounce squeeze bottle of clear vinegar
container for dumping unwanted liquids
medicine cups or baby food jars

empty, clear plastic vials   container of water for rinsing
2 plastic coffee stirrers   water

A C T I V I T Y   **1**

How Can You Make the Blue Solution Change Colors?

CAUTION: Do not taste or smell liquids.

WHAT TO DO

▼ Fill two small cups halfway to the top with the blue BTB solution.

▼ Add one drop of vinegar to cup A.
▼ Use the plastic stirring rod to mix the vinegar with the BTB.

OBSERVING   **What did you observe?**

▼ Add one drop of liquid ammonia to cup B.
▼ Use a clean stirrer to mix the liquid ammonia with the BTB.

OBSERVING   **What color change did you observe?**

▼ If no change was observed, add up to 6 more drops, one at a time; stir the solution after you add each drop.

HINT: If you are using medicine droppers, be careful to use one dropper for vinegar and another for ammonia.

OBSERVING	**What color change did you observe?**
HYPOTHESIZING	**Now, how can you make the BTB in cup B turn yellow?**
APPLYING	*Try it!*
OBSERVING	**How many drops did it take to turn cup B yellow?**
RELATING	**What reasons can you give for your observations?**
COMMUNICATING	**How did you change the color in cup B yellow?**
HYPOTHESIZING	**How can you make the BTB in cup A turn back to blue?**
APPLYING	*Try it!*

▼ How did you do it? (*Verifying*)
▼ Now, see if you can make the blue BTB in cups A and B turn yellow.

COMMUNICATING   **What have you learned about BTB so far?**

TEACHER BACKGROUND INFORMATION

Bromothymol blue Solution (BTB) is an indicator used to test for the presence of acids and bases. A BTB solution can be made by adding enough of the concentrated BTB liquid or powder to a quart (or liter) of water to turn the liquid dark blue. The concentrated BTB powder is available through scientific supply houses. The BTB liquid is usually available in pet stores in the aquarium section.

ACTIVITY **2**

Which Substances Change the Color of BTB?

MATERIALS

containers with small amounts of test solutions such as Coke, milk, fruit juices, coffee, tea
containers with small amounts of test substances such as salt, sugar, aspirin tablets, vitamin C tablets, baking soda;
container for dumping unwanted liquids (labeled *Dump Bucket*)
one pint (500 ml) bromothymol blue solution(BTB)
container of water for rinsing (labeled *Rinse Water*)

water   empty vials, medicine cups, or baby food jars
plastic coffee stirrers   medicine droppers

WHAT TO DO

Some stores sell a blue liquid called bromothymol blue (BTB).

HYPOTHESIZING   **Why do you think people buy BTB?**

▼ To find out, examine the substances you have on your table. Remember how vinegar and ammonia changed the color of BTB?

HYPOTHESIZING   **How do you think each of the new substances will affect the color of BTB?**
RECORDING DATA   **Record your guesses (hypotheses) in a chart (like the one below).**
APPLYING   **Test each substance by adding up to ten drops to blue BTB.**

▼ When testing powders and tablets, dissolve each in a small amount of water.
▼ Then add the solution, drop by drop, to the BTB.

▼ If no color change is observed, add up to ten drops of the substance to a cup of yellow BTB (see picture above).
▼ Record observations in a chart (like the one below).

TEST SUBSTANCES	HYPOTHESIS		OBSERVATIONS		
	I think the color of Blue BTB will		I observed the BTB change from		
	Stay Blue	Turn Yellow	Blue to Yellow	Yellow to Blue	Did not Change
ORANGE JUICE					
COFFEE					
COKE					
TEA					
ASPIRIN					
SALT					
SUGAR					
BAKING SODA					
APPLE JUICE					
GRAPE JUICE					
MILK					
VITAMIN C					

CATEGORIZING	**Which substances turned blue BTB to yellow?**
COMPARING	**How are these substances alike?**
CATEGORIZING	**What name can we give to these substances?**
CATEGORIZING	**Which substances turned yellow BTB to blue?**
COMPARING	**How are these substances alike?**
CATEGORIZING	**What name can we give to these substances?**
CATEGORIZING	**Which substances did not change the color of BTB?**
COMPARING	**How are these substances alike?**
CATEGORIZING	**What name can we give to these substances?**
APPLYING	**What other substances would you like to test?**
APPLYING	***Try them!***

▼ Predict how each will affect the color of BTB. (*Predicting*)
▼ Test the substances that you have chosen and see if your predictions were correct. (*Applying*)
▼ Add your observations to the chart.

> **IMPORTANT:** Be careful to avoid any strong chemicals such as bleach Draino, Saniflush, Liquid Plumber, muriatic acid, and so on.

RELATING	**From your observations, why do you think people buy BTB?**
PREDICTING	**What kind of stores do you think would sell BTB?**

TEACHER BACKGROUND INFORMATION

Some solutions (acidic solutions) change blue BTB to yellow. Other solutions (basic and neutral solutions) do not change the color when added to blue BTB. To discover if these solutions will change yellow BTB to blue, students must prepare a yellow BTB solution. This can easily be done by adding a small drop of vinegar to a small medicine cup half-filled with blue BTB solution. When a baking soda powder solution (or another basic solution) is added, the yellow color will change to blue. A neutral solution, like salt water or sugar water, will not change BTB from blue to yellow or yellow to blue. Note that the introduction of the concepts of acid, base, and neutral substance (Concept Introduction) is found at the end of this activity. Substances that turn BTB from blue to yellow are called *acids;* substances that turn BTB from yellow to blue are called *bases.* Substances that do not change the color of blue or yellow BTB are called *neutral.* The BTB solution is neutral when the color is a light green. While students have made all the observations and identified relationships, they probably will not offer the labels of *acid, base,* and *neutral* substance.

Your role is to introduce a concept label, like acid, at the appropriate time in the instructional sequence. Students might suggest that pet stores and swimming pool stores might sell BTB (or a similar indicator) to test the acidity of the water in an aquarium or swimming pool.

ACTIVITY **3**

How Can You Change the Color of Litmus Paper?

MATERIALS

dropper bottles or small containers of vinegar, ammonia, water, and other acids and bases
empty vials, cups, or baby food jars
4 strips of red litmus paper
container of water for rinsing
4 strips of blue litmus paper
medicine droppers

WHAT TO DO

▼ Get a strip of red and a strip of blue litmus paper.
▼ Place a small drop of vinegar on the end of each strip.

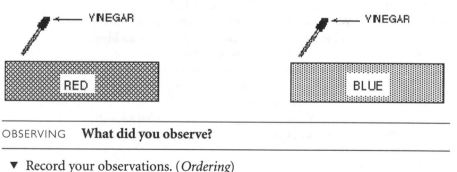

OBSERVING **What did you observe?**

▼ Record your observations. (*Ordering*)
▼ Use the same two strips of litmus paper.
▼ Place a small drop of ammonia on the unused end of each strip.

OBSERVING **What did you observe?**

▼ Record your observations. (*Recording Data*)
▼ Try distilled water next. Place a small drop of distilled water on a new strip of red litmus paper, and place another small drop on a new strip of blue litmus paper.

OBSERVING **What did you observe?**

▼ Record your observations. (*Communicating*)
▼ Now test the remaining substances, and record your observations.(*Applying*)

RELATING	**How does litmus paper react to acidic solutions?**
RELATING	**How does litmus paper react to basic solutions?**
CATEGORIZING	**What are solutions called that don't change the color of red or blue litmus paper?**

Both BTB and litmus paper are called *indicators*. Indicators are substances that help identify other substances.

CATEGORIZING	**What are the substances that litmus paper identifies?**
APPLYING	**Why do you think some stores sell litmus paper?**
PREDICTING	**How do you think that a red spot on blue litmus paper could be changed back to blue?**
PREDICTING	**How do you think that a blue spot on red litmus paper could be changed back to red?**
APPLYING	***Try it!***
INFERRING	**What conclusion can you give for what happened?**

TEACHER BACKGROUND INFORMATION

Litmus paper is an indicator that contains a chemical that reacts to acids and bases by changing color. Acids change blue litmus paper to red; whereas, bases change red litmus paper to blue. Neutral substances will not change the color of either red or blue litmus paper. Litmus paper can often be changed back to its original color. For example, blue litmus paper that has been changed to red will change back to blue if a strong enough base is added to the paper.

ACTIVITY 4

How Can You Make Your Own Indicators?

MATERIALS

bucket for dumping (labeled *Dump Bucket*)
bucket for rinsing (labeled *Rinse Bucket*)

hot water from the faucet	ammonia
vinegar	spoons
purple cabbage leaves	2 Ex-lax tablets (non-chocolate)
flower petals	blueberries
red or purple grape juice	medicine droppers
baby food jars or vials	water
3 coffee filters	

WHAT TO DO

Acid-base indicators can be made from a variety of substances. In this activity you will try to make indicators from two substances—purple cabbage leaves and Ex-lax tablets (non-chocolate variety). You may try to make other indicators from blueberries, grape juice, and flower petals as your time permits.

PURPLE CABBAGE LEAVES

▼ Cut 3-4 whole purple cabbage leaves into small pieces.
▼ Place them in a pan of boiling water for about 15 minutes or until the water is a dark color.
▼ The cabbage juice can now be used to check for acids and bases.

NOTE: You may need to add water to the cabbage juice to lighten the color so that any color changes with the vinegar or ammonia will be easier to observe.

NOTE: Do not use the chocolate variety of Ex-lax.

▼ Pour a small amount of the cabbage juice into 2 small medicine cups or jars.
▼ Add drops of vinegar to one cup of cabbage juice.
▼ Add drops of ammonia to the other cup of juice.
▼ Record your observations in a chart (like the one below). (*Recording Data*)

NON-CHOCOLATE EX-LAX

Another acid/base indicator can be made using Ex-lax tablets.
▼ Mash 2 tablets with a spoon.
▼ Add the mashed tablets to a small baby food jar filled about 2/3 full with water.
▼ Stir the solution allowing the Ex-lax tablets to dissolve.
▼ Using a coffee filter, pour the solution through the filter into an empty, clean baby food jar. This will make the solution more clear and allow any color changes to be more easily observed.
▼ This solution can now be used to check for acids and bases.
▼ Pour a small amount into each of two small medicine cups or jars.
▼ Add drops of vinegar to one cup of Ex-lax solution.
▼ Add drops of ammonia to the other cup.
▼ Record your observations in the chart. (*Recording Data*)

OTHERS

Grape juice, blueberries, and certain flower petals contain pigments that serve as acid-base indicators.
▼ To prepare a solution, mash 6–8 blueberries (or flower petals) with a spoon in a baby food jar.
▼ Fill the jar about 1/2 full of hot water and soak for 15 minutes.
▼ After the hot water has become colored, drain off the liquid.
▼ The liquid can now be used to test with vinegar and ammonia.
▼ Have students record their observations in a chart (like the one below). (*Recording Data*)

NAME OF INDICATOR	COLOR WITH ACID	COLOR WITH BASE

OBSERVING	**What color changes did you observe with each of the indicators you tested?**
COMPARING	**How are all of the acid/base indicators you have tested so far alike?**
CONTRASTING	**How are they different from each other?**
CATEGORIZING	**Based on your observations, what are some important characteristics of acid/base indicators?**
PREDICTING	**What other substances do you think might be good acid-base indicators?**
APPLYING	***Try them!***

TEACHER BACKGROUND INFORMATION

Acid-base indicators are substances that change color when mixed with acids or bases. Some indicators have dramatic color changes. Purple cabbage juice changes from reddish purple to blue green. However, the changes of other indicators are more subtle. For example, the colors of grape juice are dark purple and reddish purple. Be sure to use the non-chocolate Ex-lax tablet. The active ingredient in Ex-lax tablets is also an acid/base indicator called phenolphthalein. A phenolphthalein solution is clear when the solution becomes acidic; when the solution becomes basic, the solution turns bright pink in color.

ACTIVITY 5A
Which Liquid Contains the Most Acid?

MATERIALS (FOR A 3–4 STUDENT TEAM)

4 capped vials or jars containing a small amount of 4 different liquids—vinegar, lemon juice, orange juice, and apple juice
1 capped vial or jar of baking soda solution (dissolve 2 tablespoons in a pint of water)
container for dumping unwanted liquids (labeled *Dump Bucket*)
container of water for rinsing (labeled *Rinse Water*)
graduated 30 ml medicine cup or 50 ml cylinder
1 pint, bromothymol blue solution (BTB)

plastic, coffee stirrers
4 medicine droppers
4 vials or jars

WHAT TO DO

HYPOTHESIZING **Which of the four liquids do you think contains the most acid?**

- Label the medicine cups A, B, C, and D.
- Fill each of the 4 medicine cups with exactly 15 ml of BTB solution.
- Add *ten* drops of each of the four liquids to four different medicine cups of blue BTB solution.

RELATING **How do you think blue BTB will react to the four solutions?**

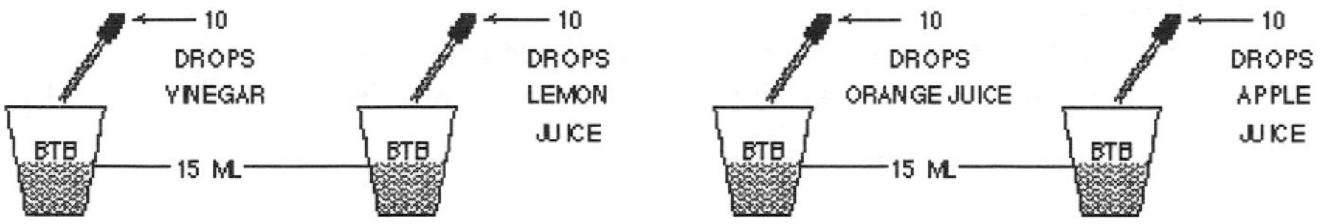

- Using the plastic stirrers, stir the solution in each medicine cup gently to mix the two liquids.

OBSERVING **What did you observe?**

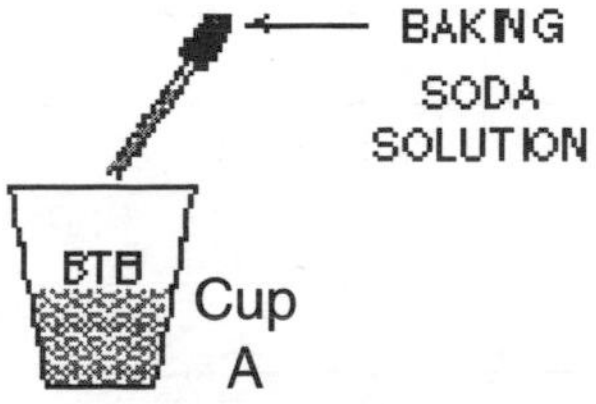

NAME OF ACID	NUMBER OF DROPS Trial 1	NUMBER OF DROPS Trial 2

▼ Now add the baking soda solution drop by drop to medicine cup A.
▼ After each drop gently stir the cup to mix the liquids.
▼ Record in a chart (like the one above) the number of drops of the baking soda solution needed to change the yellow BTB solution back to blue.(*Recording Data*)
▼ Repeat for medicine cups B, C, and D.

OBSERVING	**What do you observe happening to the color of the BTB when baking soda is added?**
SUPPORTING	**What reasons can you give for your observations?**
ORDERING	**Which acid required the most baking soda to change the color of the BTB solution?**
CATEGORIZING	**From your observations, which liquid that you tested contains the *most* acid?**
CATEGORIZING	**Which contains the *smallest* amount of acid?**
SUPPORTING	**Based on your experiments, what have you discovered about acids?**

ADDITIONAL ACTIVITIES

1. Which contains the most acid:
   a) fresh orange juice, frozen orange juice, Tang, or Awake? Which has the least?
   b) the juice from a less-ripened orange or the juice from a more-ripened orange?
   c) coffee, Sanka, tea, Coke, 7-Up, or milk? Which has the least?
2. Make a strength chart (like the one below) to show the amount of acid in all the liquids the students test.

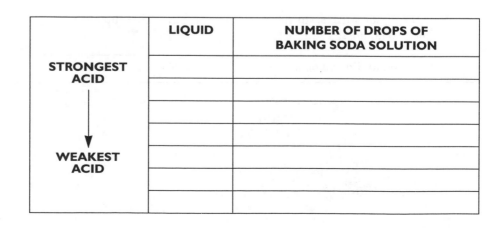

	LIQUID	NUMBER OF DROPS OF BAKING SODA SOLUTION
STRONGEST ACID		
↓		
WEAKEST ACID		

TEACHER BACKGROUND INFORMATION

Acids and bases differ in strength. Solutions differing in acid content (or strength) vary in their ability to change the color of BTB. This activity is a structured activity that allows students to examine the strength of various acids. The blue BTB solution in each vial will turn yellow as the ten drops of the acidic solution are added. When the baking soda solution just changes the yellow color back to blue, the neutral point has been reached indicating that the added acid has been neutralized. The number of drops needed to change the color to blue is an estimate of the strength of the acidity of a liquid. The estimate will be more accurate if students are advised to control variables such as the use of more than one medicine dropper (different droppers form drops of different sizes) and the angle of the medicine dropper from which the drops are added. Additional activities are suggested for students to perform at home or for a classroom learning center. If possible, save the liquids tested in this activity for use in determining their pH in Activity 6.

ACTIVITY 5B
Which Liquid Contains the Most Acid?

MATERIALS (FOR A 3–4 STUDENT TEAM)

variety of acidic solutions such as vinegar, lemon juice, orange juice, and apple juice
1 capped vial or jar of baking soda solution (dissolve 60 ml—2 tablespoons in 500 ml or a pint of water)
container for dumping unwanted liquids (labeled *Dump Bucket*)
graduated 30 ml medicine cups or 50 ml graduated cylinder
container of water for rinsing (labeled *Rinse Water*)
1 pint (500 ml) bromothymol blue solution (BTB)
vials or jars
medicine droppers

WHAT TO DO

You have learned how to test for acids and bases.

ORDERING **Which acids are stronger than other acids?**

▼ Select four acidic solutions.
▼ Design an experiment to find out which solution is the most acidic.(*Applying*)
▼ Describe your experiment.(*Communicating*)
▼ Make a chart for your data. (*Communicating*)

CATEGORIZING **Which solution contains the *most* acid?**
CATEGORIZING **Which solution contains the *least* acid?**
SUPPORTING **Based on your experiments, what have you discovered about acids?**

TEACHER BACKGROUND INFORMATION

This activity is similar to Activity 5A; however, it is less structured. Students must devise their own means of determining the strength of various acids. The activity may be used in place of Activity 5A, or it may be used after Activity 5A with different substances. For example, the students could test the amount of acid in different brands of orange juice, apple juice, coffee, or tea.

ACTIVITY 6

How Can You Determine the Strength of an Acid Using pH Paper?

MATERIALS

containers with small amounts of test solutions such as Coke, milk, fruit juices, coffee, tea, water
container for dumping unwanted liquids (labeled *Dump Bucket*)
container of water for rinsing (labeled *Rinse Water*)
empty vials, cups, or baby food jars

pH paper   medicine droppers

WHAT TO DO

The paper you will be using is called pH paper. The pH paper contains different indicators that help tell the strength of an acid or base. Different colors indicate different strengths of acids or bases (refer to the color chart on the pH paper container).

▼ Examine the liquids you have on your table.

PREDICTING   **How do you think each of the substances will affect the color of the pH paper ?**

▼ Put your predictions in order from strongest to weakest in the chart below. (*Ordering*)
▼ Place a small drop of liquid on a small piece of the pH paper.

OBSERVING   **What do you observe happening to the pH paper?**

▼ Compare the color of the pH paper to the color chart that came with the paper. (*Comparing*)

OBSERVING   **What is the color of the pH paper that you added acid to?**

▼ Find the number that goes with the color of the pH paper.

OBSERVING   **What is the pH number for the liquid that you tested?**

▼ Record the color of the pH paper and the number of that color in a chart (like the one below). (*Communicating*)

	MY PREDICTIONS	WHAT I OBSERVED	
	TEST SUBSTANCES	COLOR OF PH PAPER	PH NUMBER
STRONGEST ACID			
WEAKEST ACID			

COMPARING   **How did your predictions compare with your observations ?**

The number 7 indicates a neutral substance. Numbers above 7 indicate bases, and numbers below 7 indicate acids.

CATEGORIZING	**Which liquid do you think is most acidic?**
CATEGORIZING	**Which liquid do you think is least acidic?**
INFERRING	**What conclusion can you give for the different colors and numbers for each liquid tested?**
APPLYING	**Why do you think people use pH paper?**

▼ Make a new strength chart (like the one below) to show the acidity of each liquid you tested.

	pH NUMBER	TEST LIQUID
STRONGEST ACID ⬇ **WEAKEST ACID**		

▼ Explain how pH paper indicates the strength of an acid. *(Relating and Communicating)*

APPLYING	**What other substances would you like to test?**
APPLYING	***Try them!***

ADDITIONAL ACTIVITIES

1. How does water affect the strength of an acid? To find out, add 10 drops of vinegar or another acid to different volumes of water. Test the solutions with pH paper. Record your data in a strength chart that shows the pH of each solution.

2. How does water affect the strength of a base? To find out, add 10 drops of ammonia to different volumes of water. Test the solutions with pH paper. Record your data in a strength chart that shows the pH of each solution.

3. How can pH paper be used to determine the pH of different samples of soil? Of different samples of rain water?

4. How can you make a solution that tests neutral with pH paper? Select an acid, such as vinegar, and a base, such as baking soda mixed with distilled water. Add the acid and base together in different proportions until the resulting solution tests neutral on the pH paper.

TEACHER BACKGROUND INFORMATION

Acids and bases differ in strength. Solutions differing in acid content (or strength) vary in their ability to change the color of chemically treated paper called pH paper. The pH paper changes to various colors depending on the strength of the acid or base it is exposed to. The colors of the pH paper are compared to a chart of colors that indicates a pH number. The number 7 is neutral on the pH scale. Any reading below 7 indicates an acid; whereas, any number above 7 indicates a base. The farther from 7 the number is the stronger is the acid or base. For example, an acid with the number 2 on the pH scale is a stronger acid than an acid with the number 5, and a base with the number 13 is a stronger base than a base with the number 9. Following is a chart of the approximate pH of some common substances:

Substance	pH
Hydrochloric acid (muratic acid)	1.0 Acids
Stomach acid (contains hydrochloric acid)	2.0
Lemon juice (contains citric acid)	2.3
Vinegar (contains acetic acid)	2.9
Soft drink (contains carbonic acid)	3.0
Apple (contains malic acid)	3.1
Grapefruit (contains citric acid)	3.1
Orange (contains citric acid)	3.4
Tomato	4.3
Potato	5.8
Milk	6.7
Distilled water	7.0 Neutral
Tears	7.5 Bases
Eggs	7.8
Seawater	8.0
Milk of magnesia (magnesium hydroxide)	10.5
Lye (sodium hydroxide)	13.0

ACTIVITY (7)

What Is the Best Tablet for an Upset Stomach?

MATERIALS

4 clear, plastic vials, graduated 30 ml medicine cups, or small baby food jars
4 different tablets commonly taken for upset stomachs (Tums, Rolaids, Maalox, Bisodol, and so on)
mortar and pestle (or spoon and bowl)
25 ml graduated cylinder (optional)
jar, vial, or dropper bottle of vinegar
1 pint (500 ml) blue BTB solution

medicine dropper   plastic coffee stirrers

WHAT TO DO

People can buy tablets called antacids at drugstores and other stores. Examples of antacid tablets are Tums, Rolaids, and Maalox. When tested with BTB or other acid/base indicators, antacids are found to be *bases*. Some people use antacids when they have an upset stomach. Antacids help to "neutralize" extra acid that might be causing their stomach to be upset.

PREDICTING   **What do you think will happen to the color of a blue BTB solution when a Tums tablet is added and dissolves in the BTB?**

▼ To find out, use a mortar and pestle (or a spoon and a bowl) to crush one Tums tablet.
▼ Add all of the Tums powder to a medicine cup, clear vial, or small baby food jar that contains exactly 15 ml of the blue BTB solution.

OBSERVING   **What happened to the color of the blue BTB?**
INFERRING   **What conclusion can you give for what you observed?**
CATEGORIZING   **Which antacid do you think will "neutralize" the most acid and be the best for an upset stomach?**

▼ To find out, use a mortar and pestle (or a spoon and a bowl) and crush each of the other tablets you want to test.
▼ Add each crushed tablet to a vial, medicine cup, or small baby food jar containing exactly 15 ml of the blue BTB solution.
▼ Now add vinegar, drop by drop, to each of the four containers.

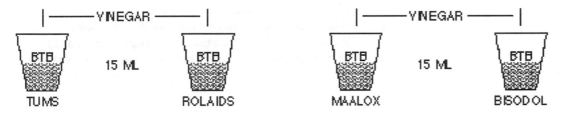

TUMS   ROLAIDS   MAALOX   BISODOL

▼ After each drop, gently stir the solution to mix the vinegar with the BTB.
▼ Record in a chart (like the one below) the total number of drops of vinegar needed to change the blue BTB to yellow (neutralize the antacid) for each of the four antacid solutions. (*Communicating*)

NOTE: Gently stir the yellow solution for about 30 seconds to make sure that the yellow BTB stays yellow.

RELATING   **What reasons can you give for any color changes you observe from yellow back to blue?**

Some tablets seem to absorb acid over a period of time.
▼ Continue to add vinegar drop by drop until the BTB *stays* yellow in each vial.
▼ In your chart, record the total number of drops needed to make each solution *stay* yellow. (*Communicating*)
▼ Use the data in your observation chart to make a bar graph set up like the one below. (*Communicating*)

NAME OF INDICATOR	NUMBER NEEDED TO CHANGE	NUMBER NEEDED TO STAY
TUMS		

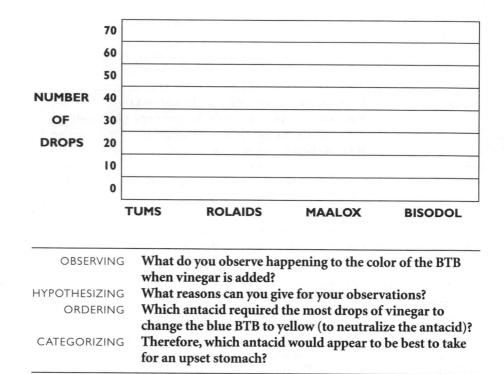

	OBSERVING	What do you observe happening to the color of the BTB when vinegar is added?
	HYPOTHESIZING	What reasons can you give for your observations?
	ORDERING	Which antacid required the most drops of vinegar to change the blue BTB to yellow (to neutralize the antacid)?
	CATEGORIZING	Therefore, which antacid would appear to be best to take for an upset stomach?

TEACHER BACKGROUND INFORMATION

This activity is a structured activity that tests various antacid tablets to determine which tablet neutralizes the most acid. The tablet that required the most drops of vinegar to stay yellow could be considered the best antacid tablet for an upset stomach. The number of drops needed to change the color to yellow is an estimate of the strength of the antacid. The estimate will be more accurate if students are advised to control variables such as the size of the drops of vinegar (by using the same medicine dropper and holding the dropper at the same angle). Avoid using Digel or other tablets that do not readily dissolve in water. Also avoid fruit flavored antacids; stick with the "original" Tums, Rolaids, and Maalox tablets.

Like Activity 5-A, this activity could be modified to a less-structured format. Students could devise their own experiment to determine which antacid will absorb the most acid (which is best for an upset stomach). The less-structured format could be used in place of Activity 7 or it may be used after Activity 7 using different antacids.

ACTIVITY **8**

How Will an Alka-Seltzer Tablet Affect the Color of BTB?

MATERIALS

clear plastic or glass container filled about 1/3 full of blue BTB solution
Alka-Seltzer tablet

WHAT TO DO

Alka-Seltzer tablets are sold as an antacid like Tums and Rolaids tablets.

SUPPORTING   **Why do we call these tablets "antacids?"**

PREDICTING   **What do you think will happen to the color of blue BTB when an Alka-Seltzer tablet is added?**

▼ Drop an Alka-Seltzer tablet into a glass container 1/3 full of blue BTB.

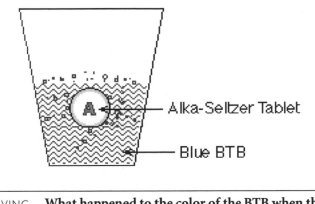

Alka-Seltzer Tablet

Blue BTB

OBSERVING   **What happened to the color of the BTB when the Alka-Seltzer tablet was added?**

HYPOTHESIZING/   **What reasons can you give for this observation?**
RELATING

RELATING   **From your observations, if Alka-Seltzer is an antacid, how can it help an upset stomach?**

TEACHER BACKGROUND INFORMATION

Students should predict that the color of BTB will *not* change when the Alka-Seltzer tablet is added since Alka-Seltzer is an antacid. However, the Alka-Seltzer tablet will cause the BTB to change to yellow. This puzzling observation (a discrepant event) can serve as a focus for a future activity: investigating the properties of Alka-Seltzer gas (see Learning Cycle 3). It would be appropriate to use this activity as a bridge to Learning Cycle 3, in which students will investigate the properties of carbon dioxide gas. An Alka-Seltzer tablet contains acids (citric acid and aspirin) and a base (sodium bicarbonate). When the tablet is added to water, carbon dioxide is released and combines with water to form a weak acid (carbonic acid, H_2CO_3). This acid changes the blue BTB to yellow. Be sure to move the container of yellow BTB out of the sight of the students soon after the color change has occurred. As the carbon dioxide produced by the bubbling Alka-Seltzer tablet is slowly released back into the air, the color of the BTB will slowly change to green and eventually back to blue (indicating a change from an acidic solution to a neutral or basic solution). In your body the color change back to blue would occur quickly and the Alka-Seltzer solution would begin "working" as an antacid. This information should not be given to students until after the concept of carbon dioxide has been introduced in Learning Cycle 3.

Properties of Gases– Carbon Dioxide

▼

CONCEPT: *Carbon dioxide is a gas having the following properties—it turns blue bromothymol blue to yellow; it turns clear limewater to cloudy it puts out a burning splint (does not support combustion) and it is heavier than air.*

1 How does Alka-Seltzer affect bromothymol blue?

2 How does Alka-Seltzer gas affect bromothymol blue?

3 How does Alka-Seltzer gas affect limewater?

4 How does Alka-Seltzer gas affect a burning splint?

5 What happens when baking soda and vinegar are mixed?

6 How does baking soda and vinegar gas affect a burning splint?

7 How does your breath affect BTB and limewater?

8 How are all the gases alike?

9 How does carbon dioxide affect a balance?

10 Can you pour carbon dioxide?

11 What happens when hydrogen peroxide and yeast are mixed?

SUGGESTED LEARNING CYCLE SEQUENCE

Exploration Activities: Activities 1 to 7

Concept Introduction: Activity 8

Application Activities: Activities 9 to 11

INTRODUCTION

Different gases have different properties. In this Learning Cycle sequence, the properties of a common gas—carbon dioxide—are investigated. Students observe changes in two indicators (bromothymol blue and limewater). They also observe differences in how carbon dioxide and air affect a burning splint.

In the Exploration Phase, students test the properties of carbon dioxide generated in three ways: Alka-Seltzer tablet added to water, baking soda added to vinegar, and students' breath blown through a straw. In the Application Phase, students also observe another property of carbon dioxide—it is heavier than air.

The initial activity in this sequence (Activity 1) provides a problem focus (discrepant event) that was used as a puzzling final Application Phase activity in Learning Cycle 2, which investigated the properties of *acids and bases*. This activity provides an excellent bridge from Learning Cycle 2—Acids and Bases, to Learning Cycle 3—Carbon Dioxide. Unless activities involving testing carbon dioxide with BTB are eliminated, Learning Cycle 2—Acids and Bases, should serve as a prerequisite to Learning Cycle 3—Carbon Dioxide.

Based on their observations through Activity 10, many students will predict that *all* gases will turn BTB from blue to yellow, will turn limewater from clear to cloudy, and will put out a burning splint. In Activity 11, students test a new gas made by adding yeast to hydrogen peroxide. They observe *no* changes in BTB and limewater, and the burning splint burns more brightly. They infer that this gas is different from carbon dioxide. In reality, it is another common gas, *oxygen.*

The activities have been written as instructions and questions for your students and each is accompanied by background information for you. As you work with students on the activities, feel free to make use of the drawings and charts included here. You may want to recreate some of the charts on an overhead transparency or on the blackboard so your students can refer to them.

LEARNING CYCLE STRATEGY

In this sequence, the Learning Cycle is organized around the concept of carbon dioxide. Activities 1–7 represent the Exploration Phase of the Learning Cycle. The term *carbon dioxide* is introduced (Concept Introduction) in Activity 8. Activities 9–11 serve to apply and extend the concept to new situations (Application Phase). Activity 11 could serve as an initial activity in a new Learning Cycle investigating the properties of *oxygen* gas.

SAFETY

The materials used in this sequence are relatively safe. Students should wear goggles when making and testing these gases to protect them from any splattering of chemicals. If possible, plastic containers and tubes should be used to prevent any possible injury from glass particles.

MATERIALS

The following materials needed in the teaching of this Learning Cycle can be purchased from science supply companies such as Delta Education, P.O. Box M, Nashua, NH 03601–6012 (1–800–258–1302): Bromothymol blue, limewater, 250 ml plastic flasks, wooden splints.

REFERENCES

Balloons and Gases: Teacher's Guide. 1985. Elementary Science Study Series. Nashua, N.H.: Delta Education, Inc.

Beisenherz, P.C. 1981. "Fizz-fizz Science." *Science and Children* 19 (1): 30–32.

Faulkner, S.P. 1993. "Lessons with a Fizz." *The Science Teacher* 60 (1): 26–29.

Fisher, M. 1982. "Comedy with CO_2." *Science and Children* 20 (2): 36–37.

Foster, J., Mandarino, S., and Birk, J.P. 1986. "Screen for Carbon Dioxide." *The Science Teacher* 53 (7): 31–33.

Marson, R. 1978. *Oxidation: A Task Card Module.* Task Oriented Physical Science (TOPS). Canby, OR: TOPS Learning Systems.

McCarthy, F.W. 1970. "The Preparation of Oxygen." *Science and Children* 7 (7): 16–17.

Three Gases 1975. Science: A Process Approach II (Module 92). Nashua, NH: Delta Education, Inc.

Tingle, J.B. 1986. "A Plop and Fizz Lab." *The Science Teacher* 53 (3): 42–43.

ACTIVITY ①

How Does Alka-Seltzer Affect Bromothymol Blue (BTB)?

MATERIALS

Alka-Seltzer tablet
BTB solution

clear plastic or glass container

WHAT TO DO

Earlier in your study of *acids and bases* (see Learning Cycle 2), you learned that Alka-Seltzer is called an antacid. This means that when you test Alka-Seltzer with an acid-base indicator such as BTB, the color of the indicator should identify it as a base. Some people take Alka-Seltzer to help neutralize extra acid that will perhaps help to relieve their upset stomach.

PREDICTING   **What do you think will happen to the color of the blue BTB solution when an Alka-Seltzer tablet is added?**

▼ Drop an Alka-Seltzer tablet into a jar half-filled with blue BTB.

OBSERVING   **What happened to the color of the blue BTB solution?**
HYPOTHESIZING   **What reasons can you give for your observation?**
INFERRING   **From your observations in earlier activities, if Alka-Seltzer is supposed to be an antacid, how can it help an upset stomach?**

TEACHER BACKGROUND INFORMATION

This activity provides an excellent bridge from Learning Cycle 2—Acids and Bases. Students should observe that the BTB immediately turns yellow when the Alka-Seltzer is added. This is a discrepant event because antacids should keep BTB blue. Students should be encouraged to hypothesize why the BTB turned yellow when no closure was achieved. In addition to the chemicals found in an Alka-Seltzer tablet, the teacher can guide students to the hypothesis that the gas produced might have caused the color change. They might be asked to design an experiment to find out. Activity 2 provides one such experiment.

MATERIALS

one 250 ml flask   1 stopper with hole
Alka-Seltzer tablet   water
BTB solution   12-inch piece of aquarium tubing

WHAT TO DO

▼ Put one end of the aquarium tubing just through the stopper (see picture).
▼ Put the other end of the tube into a small jar of BTB solution.
▼ Fill the flask about ⅓ full of water.
▼ Add ½ of an Alka-Seltzer tablet to the water.
▼ Quickly, place the stopper tightly into the flask.

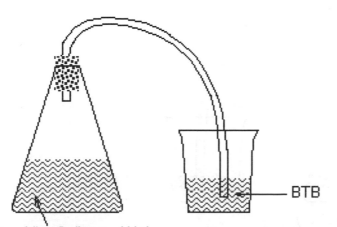

BTB

Alka-Seltzer + Water

OBSERVING	What changes do you observe inside the flask?
HYPOTHESIZING	Based on your hypothesis in Activity 1, what do you think will happen to the BTB when Alka-Seltzer gas is bubbled into the BTB?
OBSERVING/COMPARING AND CONTRASTING	What changes do you observe in the color of the BTB solution?
INFERRING	What conclusion can you offer for your observations?

TEACHER BACKGROUND INFORMATION

Students should observe that when only the gas is bubbled into the blue BTB, the BTB turns yellow. If no other contamination (Alka-Seltzer solution) enters the BTB solution, students can infer that the color change is due to the gas. As students do not know at this point that Alka-Seltzer gas is carbon dioxide, an explanation of the chemical reaction is not appropriate. If and when appropriate, students can be given the information that carbon dioxide and water combine to form a weak acid (carbonic acid) which is unstable. Over time the yellow color will change back to blue because the carbonic acid is changing back to carbon dioxide and escaping out of the solution into the air. The reaction is as follows: $CO_2 + H_2O \rightarrow H_2CO_3$ (carbonic acid).

ACTIVITY **3**

How Does Alka-Seltzer Gas Affect Limewater?

MATERIALS

12-inch piece of aquarium tubing

one 250 ml Flask	1 stopper with hole
Alka-Seltzer tablet	water
30 ml limewater	

WHAT TO DO

▼ Put one end of the aquarium tubing just through the stopper (see picture).
▼ Put the other end of the tube into a small jar containing 30 ml of limewater.
▼ Fill the flask about ⅓ full of water.
▼ Add ½ of an Alka-Seltzer tablet to the water.
▼ Quickly, place the stopper tightly into the flask.

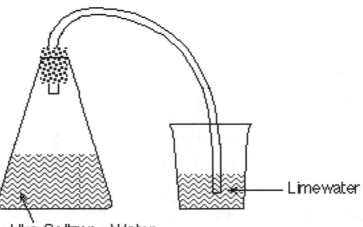

Limewater

Alka-Seltzer + Water

OBSERVING/COMPARING   **What changes do you observe in the limewater?**
AND CONTRASTING

SUPPORTING   **What reasons can you offer for your observations?**

TEACHER BACKGROUND INFORMATION

Students should observe that when the gas is bubbled into a clear solution of lime-water, the solution should turn milky or cloudy. Limewater can be made by adding 1–2 teaspoons of calcium hydroxide (lime) to a quart of water. Shake and allow to set overnight. Pour the clear solution into a clean jar with a lid. Store the limewater until needed. As the students do not know at this point that Alka-Seltzer gas is carbon dioxide (CO_2), an explanation of the chemical reaction is not appropriate. If and when appropriate, students can be given the information that calcium hydroxide and carbon dioxide react to form calcium carbonate which is an insoluble, white compound that makes the limewater solution look cloudy.
$Ca(OH)_2 + CO_2 \rightarrow CaCO_3 + H_2O$

<table>
<tr><td>ACTIVITY 4
How Does Alka-Seltzer Gas Affect a Burning Splint?</td></tr>
</table>

MATERIALS

12-inch piece of aquarium tubing
dishpan or container of water (9 × 9-inch cake pan or larger)
1 small baby food jar or plastic vial with lid

one 250 ml flask	1 stopper with hole
water	Alka-Seltzer tablet
wooden splint	matches

WHAT TO DO

▼ Fill a dishpan or large container ¾ full of water.
▼ Fill a baby food jar or plastic vial with water and turn it upside down in the pan of water.
▼ Put one end of the aquarium tubing barely through the stopper (see picture).
▼ Put the other end of the tube inside the baby food jar (see picture).
▼ Fill the flask about ⅓ full of water.
▼ Add one Alka-Seltzer tablet to the water in the flask.

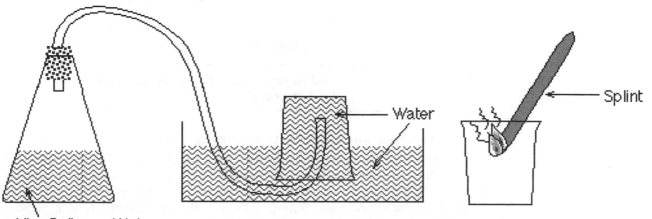

Alka-Seltzer + Water   Water   Splint

OBSERVING/COMPARING
AND CONTRASTING
What changes do you observe inside the baby food jar?

▼ Leave the tube inside the baby food jar until the Alka-Seltzer gas pushes out all the water.
▼ Add another Alka-Seltzer tablet if necessary.
▼ When all of the water is out of the baby food jar, use the lid to tightly close the jar.
▼ Take the jar out of the water and turn it right side up.
▼ Light a wooden splint.
▼ Quickly unscrew the lid and place the burning end of the splint into the jar.

OBSERVING
What happens to the flame of the burning splint when you put it inside the jar of Alka-Seltzer gas?

OBSERVING
How long does the splint continue to burn?

▼ Now collect room air in the baby food jar or vial.
▼ Light a wooden splint.
▼ Carefully put it inside the jar or vial of air.

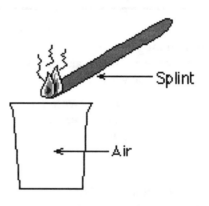

OBSERVING
What happens to the burning splint when you put it inside the jar or vial of air?

OBSERVING
How long does the splint continue to burn?

CONTRASTING
What differences did you observe between the burning splint put into the jar or vial of air and the burning splint put into the jar or vial of Alka-Seltzer gas?

INFERRING
What conclusions can you give for any differences you observed?

We have now done three tests with Alka-Seltzer gas.

CATEGORIZING
Based on your observations, what are three properties of Alka-Seltzer gas?

TEACHER BACKGROUND INFORMATION

Students should observe that while a burning splint placed in air continues to burn, the flame of a burning splint placed in Alka-Seltzer gas goes out immediately. Students should infer that Alka-Seltzer gas is different from air. Their observation that Alka-Seltzer gas puts out the burning splint immediately, indicates that this gas does not support combustion.

What Happens When Baking Soda and Vinegar Are Mixed?

MATERIALS

one 250 ml flask
baking soda
BTB solution

1 stopper with hole
vinegar
limewater solution

12-inch piece of aquarium tubing

WHAT TO DO

▼ Put one end of the aquarium tubing just through the stopper (see picture).
▼ Put the other end of the tube into a small jar of BTB solution.
▼ Add about 25 ml of vinegar to the flask.
▼ Add about 1 teaspoon of baking soda to the vinegar.
▼ Quickly, place the stopper tightly into the flask.

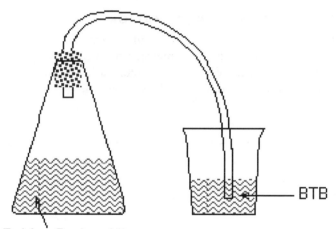

Baking Soda + Vinegar — BTB

OBSERVING/COMPARING AND CONTRASTING	**What changes do you observe inside the flask?**
OBSERVING	**What changes do you observe in the color of the BTB solution?**
INFERRING	**What conclusion can you give for your observations?**

▼ Clean your flask and add 25 ml of new fresh vinegar to the flask.
▼ Put one end of the aquarium tubing into a small jar of limewater.

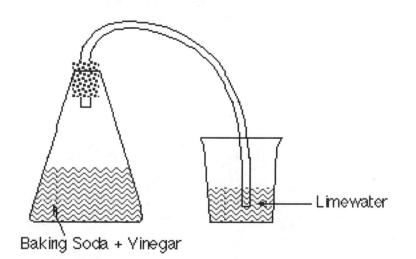

Baking Soda + Vinegar — Limewater

▼ Add about 1 teaspoon of baking soda to the vinegar and quickly place the stopper tightly into the flask.

OBSERVING/COMPARING AND CONTRASTING	**What changes do you observe in the limewater solution?**
COMPARING AND CONTRASTING	**Based on your observations of BTB and limewater, how does baking soda and vinegar gas compare with Alka-Seltzer gas?**
COMPARING	**How are the two gases alike?**
CONTRASTING	**How are they different?**
CATEGORIZING	**What other liquids besides vinegar could you add to baking soda to make a gas that produces the changes you observed in BTB and limewater?**

▼ Design an experiment to find out. (*Applying*)

TEACHER BACKGROUND INFORMATION

Students should observe that baking soda and vinegar gas (CO_2) will turn blue BTB to a yellow color, and it will turn limewater from clear to cloudy. When students add acids (vinegar, fruit juices, or hydrochloric acid) to baking soda, a chemical change occurs in which carbon dioxide is produced.

ACTIVITY 6

How Does Baking Soda and Vinegar Gas Affect a Burning Splint?

MATERIALS

dishpan or container of water (9 × 9-inch cake pan or larger)
1 small baby food jar or plastic vial with lid.
12-inch piece of aquarium tubing

1 flask	1 stopper with hole
vinegar	baking soda
wooden splint	matches

WHAT TO DO

▼ Fill a dishpan or large container ¾ full of water.
▼ Fill a baby food jar with water and turn it upside down in the pan of water.
▼ Put one end of the aquarium tubing barely through the stopper (see picture).
▼ Put the other end of the tube inside the baby food jar (see picture).
▼ Add about 25 ml of vinegar to the flask.
▼ Add about 1 teaspoon of baking soda to the vinegar.
▼ Quickly, place the stopper tightly into the flask.

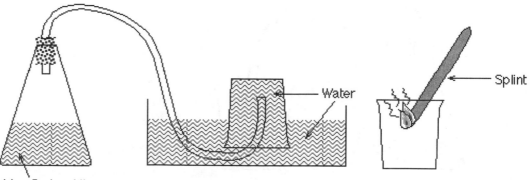

Baking Soda + Vinegar   Water   Splint

▼ Leave the tube inside the baby food jar until the baking soda and vinegar gas pushes out all the water.

▼ You may need to add more baking soda and vinegar to the flask to get more gas.

▼ When all of the water is out of the jar, use the lid to tightly close the baby food jar or vial.

▼ Take the jar or vial out of the water and turn it right side up.

▼ Light a wooden splint.

▼ Quickly unscrew the lid and place the burning end of the splint in the jar.

RELATING	**What happens to the flame of the burning splint when you put it inside the jar or vial of baking soda and vinegar gas?**
OBSERVING	**How long does the splint continue to burn?**
COMPARING AND CONTRASTING	**How does this observation compare with your observations of the burning splint in room air?**
COMPARING AND CONTRASTING	**How does this observation compare with your observations of the burning splint in Alka-Seltzer gas?**
INFERRING	**What conclusion can you give from your observations?**

TEACHER BACKGROUND INFORMATION

Students should observe that baking soda and vinegar gas (CO_2) puts out the burning splint immediately, demonstrating that this gas does not support combustion.

MATERIALS

1 soda straw
limewater solution

BTB solution
2 baby food jars

WHAT TO DO

▼ Fill one baby food jar half-full of BTB solution and half-full of limewater.

PREDICTING	**What will happen to the color of the BTB when you blow into the BTB using the straw?**
APPLYING	*Try it!*

▼ Continue to blow into the BTB for about 1 minute.

▼ Be careful not to blow too hard as you might blow the BTB out of the cup.

OBSERVING	**What do you observe?**
PREDICTING	**What will happen to the limewater solution when you blow into it using the straw?**
OBSERVING	**What do you observe?**
INFERRING	**What conclusion can you offer from your observations?**
COMPARING AND CONTRASTING	**Based on your observations with BTB and limewater, how does your breath compare with Alka-Seltzer gas and baking soda and vinegar gas?**

TEACHER BACKGROUND INFORMATION

When students blow their breath into BTB, they should observe the color changing to yellow. When their breath is blown into limewater, the solution should turn cloudy. Compared to air, their breath contains a higher percentage of CO_2.

<table>
<tbody>
<tr><td>

ACTIVITY 8

How Are All the Gases Alike?

</td></tr>
</tbody>
</table>

MATERIALS

WHAT TO DO

So far, you have made gases three different ways.

CATEGORIZING	**What are the three ways?**
COMPARING	**How are the gases alike?**
CONTRASTING	**How are the gases different?**
CATEGORIZING	**What is the name of the gas that has these properties?**
HYPOTHESIZING	**What are some other ways of making the same gas?**
CATEGORIZING	**For example, does a burning candle produce a gas? Does soda water produce a gas? Does dry ice produce a gas?**
COMMUNICATING	**What are the properties of these gases?**
APPLYING	**Design investigations to find out.**

TEACHER BACKGROUND INFORMATION

In this activity, the concept of carbon dioxide is introduced (Concept Introduction). Students are asked to identify the various common attributes or properties of the gases they have made. If the students cannot name the gas as carbon dioxide, the teacher can supply the name or label.

ACTIVITY 9

How Will Carbon Dioxide Affect a Balance?

MATERIALS

2 identical half-gallon empty plastic milk cartons

meter stick	string
2 identical paper lunch bags	baking soda
vinegar	thumbtacks or staples

WHAT TO DO

▼ Hang the meter stick by a string attached at the middle (50 cm mark).
▼ Use thumbtacks or staples to attach the lunch bags to the ends of the meter stick. Be sure to attach the two bags so they are open wide as they hang on the meter stick.
▼ Move the piece of string around until the sacks are balanced.

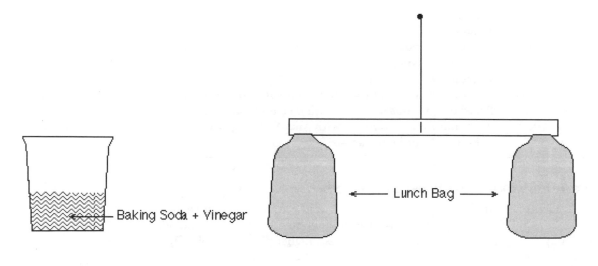

Baking Soda + Vinegar

Lunch Bag

HYPOTHESIZING	**What do you think will happen to the balance when you "pour" air from an empty jar into one of the bags?**

▼ "Pour" air from one of the milk cartons into one of the sacks.

OBSERVING	**What do you observe?**
HYPOTHESIZING	**What do you think will happen to the balance when you "pour" carbon dioxide from the jar into one of the bags?**

▼ Add enough baking soda and vinegar to another milk carton to make a full carton of carbon dioxide gas.

▼ "Pour" *only* the carbon dioxide gas from the carton into the other sack on the balance.

OBSERVING	**What do you observe?**
INFERRING	**What conclusion can you offer from your observations?**

TEACHER BACKGROUND INFORMATION

Students should observe that the bag containing the carbon dioxide is heavier, thus causing the balance to move.

ACTIVITY 10

Can You "Pour" Carbon Dioxide?

MATERIALS

aluminum foil piece (12 inches long and 7 inches wide)
12-inch wooden ruler or substitute
one half-gallon plastic milk carton
trough built at a 45 degree angle

baking soda (3 tablespoons)	vinegar (½ pint)
oil-based clay (5 small balls)	5 birthday candles
matches	Alka-Seltzer tablets

WHAT TO DO

▼ Place a 12-inch ruler at a 45 degree angle on a table.
▼ Lay the foil on top of the ruler.
▼ Fold the foil to make a trough with at least 2 inches on each side.
▼ Tape the foil to the ruler.
▼ Use the small balls of clay to stick the 5 candles to the foil.
▼ Put the candles from the top to the bottom of the ruler.
▼ Add enough baking soda and vinegar to the empty jar to make a jar full of carbon dioxide.
▼ Light the candles.

In the last investigation, you discovered that carbon dioxide is heavier than air.

PREDICTING	**What do you think will happen to the candle flames when you "pour" the carbon dioxide out of the milk carton down the trough?**
APPLYING	***Try it!***
OBSERVING	**What do you observe?**
SUPPORTING	**What reason can you give for your observations?**

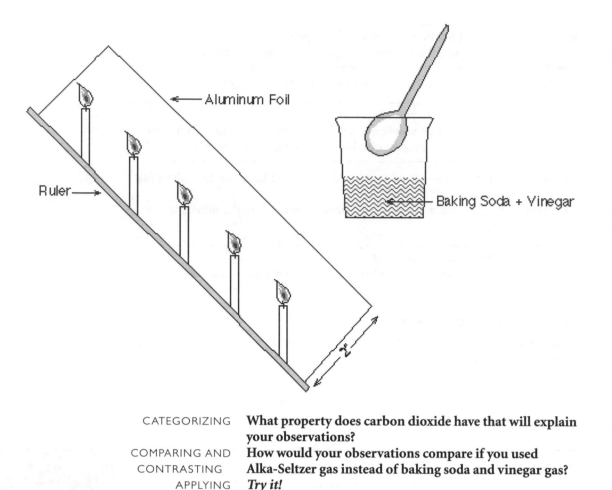

CATEGORIZING | **What property does carbon dioxide have that will explain your observations?**

COMPARING AND CONTRASTING | **How would your observations compare if you used Alka-Seltzer gas instead of baking soda and vinegar gas?**

APPLYING | ***Try it!***

TEACHER BACKGROUND INFORMATION

Students should observe that when carbon dioxide is "poured" down the trough, the candles go out one by one (starting from the top). Thus, carbon dioxide does not support combustion and is heavier than air.

ACTIVITY (11)

What Happens When Hydrogen Peroxide and Yeast Are Mixed?

MATERIALS

one plastic flask or container (250–400 ml)
30 ml limewater, 30ml BTB solution
1 small bottle hydrogen peroxide

12-inch aquarium tubing   1 stopper with hole
1 package dry yeast   baby food jar

WHAT TO DO

▼ Put one end of the aquarium tubing through the hole in the rubber stopper.
▼ Put ¼ teaspoon of yeast into the flask. Add 25 ml of hydrogen peroxide.
▼ Quickly, put the stopper tightly into the flask.
▼ Place the other end of the aquarium tubing into a small baby food jar half-filled with limewater solution.

HYPOTHESIZING | **What do you think will happen to the limewater?**

APPLYING | ***Try it!***

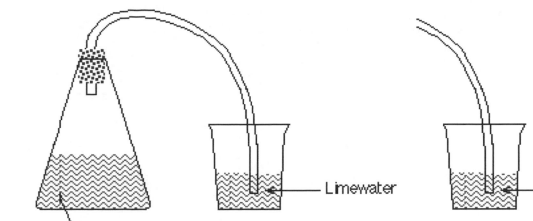

Yeast + Hydrogen Peroxide

Limewater

BTB

OBSERVING/COMPARING AND CONTRASTING	**What changes do you observe inside the flask?**
OBSERVING	**What do you observe in the flask containing the yeast and hydrogen peroxide?**
OBSERVING/COMPARING AND CONTRASTING	**What changes do you observe in the limewater solution?**

▼ Quickly, take the end of the tubing out of the limewater and put it into a small baby food jar half-filled with blue BTB.

OBSERVING/COMPARING AND CONTRASTING	**What changes do you observe in the color of the BTB solution?**
RELATING	**What happens to the flame of a burning splint when you put it inside a vial filled with this gas?**
APPLYING	***Try it!*** **(See Activities 4 and 6)**
COMPARING AND CONTRASTING	**Based on your observations of BTB, limewater, and a burning splint, how does the gas made by adding hydrogen peroxide to yeast compare with carbon dioxide gas?**

TEACHER BACKGROUND INFORMATION

Hydrogen peroxide and yeast gas (oxygen) will *not* make the limewater cloudy or change the color of blue BTB to yellow. The formation of calcium carbonate ($CaCO_3$), the insoluble white substance that makes the limewater cloudy, occurs only when carbon dioxide gas (CO_2) is bubbled into limewater (calcium hydroxide). The change in limewater from clear to cloudy is a specific property of carbon dioxide gas.

Expansion and Contraction of Gases

▼

CONCEPT: *When air is heated, it expands; when air is cooled, it contracts.*

1 How does a closed tube affect a flame?

2 Can you solve the case of the mysterious water?

3 How high will the water rise?

4 Who can make the water rise the highest?

5 How can you make the membrane move?

6 How can soap help you explain the mystery of the rising water?

7 How can you now explain the mystery of the rising water?

8 The mystery of the egg and the bottle (Teacher Demonstration)

9 Solve the soda can mystery! (Teacher Demonstration)

SUGGESTED LEARNING CYCLE SEQUENCE

Exploration Activities: Activities 1 to 6

Concept Introduction: Activity 7

Application Activities: Activities 8 to 9

INTRODUCTION

Most of the activities in the Exploration Phase of this Learning Cycle are based on a hands-on adaptation of a classic demonstration. When a pint or quart jar is placed over a burning candle standing in a glass pie plate filled with water, students observe water rising in the jar after the burning candle goes out. From their participation in a number of hands-on activities in this Learning Cycle, students develop an explanation of why water rises in a tube after the burning candles are extinguished. They discover that burning candles produce heat that causes the surrounding air to warm and to expand. When the source of heat is eliminated, the warm air cools and contracts, resulting in a rise of water inside the tube.

A popular student hypothesis to explain the water rise in this sequence is that the candles use up all of the oxygen in the tube and the water rises to take its place. If students are made aware that 20% of the air is oxygen, they will hypothesize that the water will rise inside the tube to occupy 20% of the total volume of the tube.

However, this explanation ignores the role of heat, which, in causing the air in the jar or tube to expand, is the major factor in the water rise. Students observe in Activity 4 that with an increased number of candles, the water rises higher in the tube (often up to 50% of the volume of the tube). This is discrepant to their initial explanation and the fact that 20% of the air is oxygen.

As the heated air expands, it exerts greater pressure and some of it is "pushed" out under the jar or tube. When the jar or tube is placed in the water covering the candles, the candles are extinguished. The smaller amount (fewer molecules) of air remaining inside the jar or tube contracts as the air cools. This creates a lower pressure inside the jar or tube and the water rises replacing the missing air.

To help students infer the higher pressure inside the jar or tube resulting from the expansion of the heated air, students perform Activity 6. They observe bubbles forming on the outside of the tube upon the addition of liquid detergent. These bubbles indicate a higher pressure *inside* the tube, which pushes the air to the outside of the tube. The higher pressure inside the tube is inconsistent with their hypothesis that the oxygen is being used up (resulting in a lowered pressure inside the tube).

In spite of their exposure to the activities in this Learning Cycle sequence, many students and adults have difficulty in letting go of their initial hypothesis to explain why the water rises inside the tube: that oxygen is being used up and water rises in the tube to replace the missing oxygen. Be aware of and sensitive to this strongly held student preconception. One way of overcoming this preconception is to provide activities using heat sources other than fire. Activity 9 provides experiences that utilize heat sources other than fire.

Also help your students get a feeling for the ocean of air that is pressing on the water in the tray. Throughout the Learning Cycle, help students realize that it is the air in the classroom *outside* the plastic tube, the milk bottle, and the soda can that is exerting pressure (about 15 pounds per square inch) and is causing the observed changes in the water, egg, and soda can.

LEARNING CYCLE STRATEGY

The concept—when air is heated, it expands; when cooled, it contracts—fits nicely into a Learning Cycle strategy. In this sequence, students perform Activities 1–6 in an inductive manner (Exploration Phase). Your role is to encourage students to initiate hypotheses that explain why the water rises inside the tube and to help them draw inferences based on the various observations they make in Activities 1–6. Also help students compare similarities and differences among the various activities observed. Through discussions of their observations and comparisons of the similarities and differences among the examples, the introduction of the concept can occur (Concept Introduction Phase). In this sequence, the introduction occurs in Activity 7. The remaining activities in the unit serve to reinforce and apply the concept (Application Phase).

This sequence of activities is only one of many logical sequences that could be employed. For example, you could initiate the teaching of the concept by using the egg-in-the-bottle demonstration (Activity 8). To maintain an inductive sequence where students are not given the concept (until Activity 7), the use of the egg-in-the-bottle demonstration as an initial activity should not involve providing students with any explanations of the phenomena. Students should be encouraged to observe and hypothesize. This activity can serve as an excellent motivational grabber in the sequence of activities leading up to the introduction of the concept. If a piece of burning paper is used in the egg-in-the-bottle demonstration, students are likely to come up with an explanation why the oxygen is used up. This explanation might well be extended into their observation of the water as it rises in the tube (Activity 2). This will make their observation that the water rises in the tube in excess of 20% (Activity 4) even more puzzling (a discrepant event).

The activities have been written as instructions and questions for your students, and each is accompanied by background information for you. As you work with students on the activities, feel free to make use of the drawings and charts included here. You may want to recreate some of the charts on an overhead transparency or on the blackboard so your students can refer to them.

PREREQUISITES

Before students can state that 20% of the air is oxygen, they must have received this specific information. Students could receive the information any time prior to this unit. The following activity can serve as an excellent prerequisite to provide students the observation that 20% of the air is oxygen. When a ball of wet steel wool is placed inside the plastic tube, capped, and the tube placed in a tray of water for several days, rust is formed indicating a chemical reaction between the steel wool and the oxygen gas (O_2) inside the tube. If adequate steel wool is present, all of the oxygen combines with the steel wool creating a lower pressure inside the tube. The constant pressure of the air outside the tube pushing down on the surface of the water in the tray forces the water to rise inside the tube until the air pressure is equalized. The water rises in the tube to a maximum volume of 20%. With their knowledge of the properties of nitrogen gas, and the chemical reaction between steel wool and oxygen in which the oxygen inside the tube combines with the wet steel wool to form rust, students can infer from their observations that 20% of the air is oxygen (see Learning Cycle 3—Properties of Gases). With this prerequisite activity, students will be able to predict in Activity 3 that the water will occupy about 20% of the total volume of the tube when the candle goes out.

In addition, the idea that air is a mixture should be introduced prior to this Learning Cycle sequence. Earlier exposure to the properties of carbon dioxide, oxygen, and nitrogen is also essential to the development of this concept. It is important that students have an understanding of the movement of air molecules and the relationship of their movement to air pressure; they must also be introduced to the changes occurring during the burning process.

SAFETY

You may wish to have additional adult supervision (parents, paraprofessionals) during this sequence. Students will need preparation in their handling of fire in those activities utilizing burning candles. As a safety precaution, students should use wooden matches and use them only in isolation of other matches. Students with long hair need to take precautions to prevent any accidents. When performing activities using fire, eye goggles should be available and used by you and your students.

MATERIALS

The following materials needed in the teaching of the Learning Cycle sequence can be purchased from science supply companies such as Delta Education, P.O. Box M, Nashua, NH 03061–6012 (1–800–258–1302): plastic tray, plastic tube with cap, rubber membrane, oil-based clay, safety goggles, metric rulers.

REFERENCES

Baron, J., and Teachworth, M. 1988. "Canned Heat." *Science and Children* 26 (1): 33.

Dantonio, M., and Beisenherz, P.C. 1990. "Don't Just Demonstrate—Motivate!" *The Science Teacher* 57 (2): 27–29.

Gases and "Airs": Teachers' Guide. 1985. Elementary Science Studies Series, Nashua, NH: Delta Education.

Lawson, A.E. 1995. *Science Teaching and the Development of Thinking.* Belmont, CA: Wadsworth Publishing Company.

———. 1988. "A Better Way to Teach Biology." *The American Biology Teacher* 50 (5): 266–274.

Marson, R. 1978. *Oxidation: A Task Card Module.* Task Oriented Physical Science (TOPS). Canby, OR: TOPS Learning Systems.

ACTIVITY 1

How Does a Closed Tube Affect a Flame?

MATERIALS

oil-based clay	plastic tray
large plastic tube with cap	matches
birthday candles	safety goggles

WHAT TO DO

▼ Take a ball of clay and flatten it like a pancake.

▼ The clay must be wide enough so that the tube can be put on top of the pancake and still have some clay around the outside of the tube.

▼ Set the clay pancake in the bottom of the plastic tray. Put the candle in the center of the clay pancake.

▼ Light the candle.

▼ Put the tube with the cap over the lighted candle.

▼ Try different ways of putting the tube over the candle to see the effect they have.

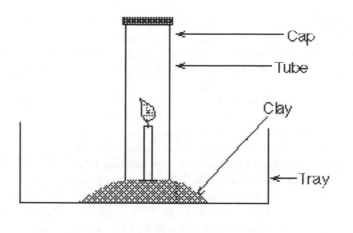

| OBSERVING | **What happens to the burning candle when you try different ways?** |
| SUPPORTING | **What reasons can you give for any differences you observe in how the candle burns?** |

TEACHER BACKGROUND INFORMATION

Students will suggest that when the tube is placed over the burning candle, the candle will go out because all the oxygen is used up. This activity is important in order to provide opportunities for students to observe differences in the behavior of a burning candle when the tube and the cap are manipulated in various ways. Students could repeat the activity, first using the tube with the cap and then without the cap, and observe differences in the burning of the candle.

ACTIVITY (2)

Can You Solve the Case of the Mysterious Water?

MATERIALS

plastic tray
birthday candles
matches
safety goggles

oil-based clay
large plastic tube with cap
water

WHAT TO DO

▼ Take a ball of clay and flatten it out like a pancake.
▼ Set the clay pancake in the bottom of the plastic tray.
▼ Fill the plastic tray with water so that the clay pancake is covered.
▼ Set the candle in the middle of the pancake.
▼ Light the candle.
▼ Lower the plastic tube *quickly* over the candle and into the water in the tray.

IMPORTANT: Do *not* put the tube tightly on the clay pancake.

OBSERVING	**What did you notice happened to the burning candle?**
OBSERVING	**What did you notice happened to the water inside the tube?**
CATEGORIZING	**Did any change you observed happen before or after the candle went out?**
HYPOTHESIZING	**What reasons can you give for your observations?**

TEACHER BACKGROUND INFORMATION

Students should observe that as the candle goes out the water rises inside the tube. Encourage students to offer hypotheses to explain the rising water. No closure should be reached at this point. Typically, students will suggest that the water rises to replace the missing air (*oxygen*) used up by the burning candle.

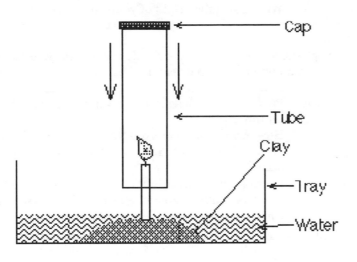

MATERIALS

plastic tray
birthday candles
matches
metric ruler

oil-based clay
large plastic tube with cap
water
safety goggles

WHAT TO DO

In the last activity (2), you observed water rising inside the tube when the tube was put in the water over the burning candle.

HYPOTHESIZING	**Based on past learning, what percentage of the total volume of the tube will the rising water occupy?**
SUPPORTING	**What reasons can you give for your hypotheses?**

Let's find out how much water will rise in the tube.

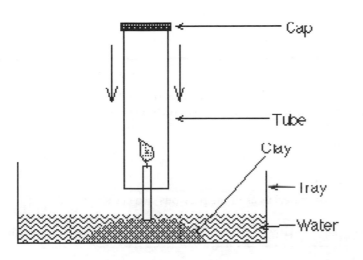

▼ Set up the materials as shown in the picture.
▼ Use your ruler to measure the height of the tube in centimeters (cm).

COMMUNICATING	**Write down the height of your tube in centimeters.**

▼ Light your candle.
▼ Lower the plastic tube *quickly* over the candle and into the water in the tray.
▼ Measure the amount of water that goes up the tube.

COMMUNICATING	**Write down the height of the water in the tube in centimeters.**
VERIFYING	**How many centimeters did the water rise in the tube?**
VERIFYING	**What percentage of the total volume of the tube is occupied by water?**
HYPOTHESIZING	**For example, if the height of the empty tube is 14 centimeters and the water rose 7 centimeters inside the tube, what would be the percentage of water inside the tube?**

(7 cm water/14 cm total tube = ½ (of the tube is occupied by water. ½ = 0.50 × 100% = 50%)

SUPPORTING	**What reasons can you give for any difference between the percentage of water in your tube and the percentage of water in the tube you hypothesized?**

TEACHER BACKGROUND INFORMATION

Students might predict that the water should rise 20% of the total volume of the tube. To make this prediction students need prerequisite information. They need to know that air is a mixture, that air is primarily nitrogen (79%) and oxygen (20%), and that nitrogen gas is largely inert and cannot be used up during the burning of the candles. Therefore, if all the oxygen is used up, the water should occupy a maximum of 20% of the tube (see the Introduction to this Learning Cycle for a description of an excellent activity to provide students the observation that 20% of the air is oxygen).

Calculating percentages will be a challenge for many students. It might be desirable to provide pictures of tubes and have students draw in their observations and calculate the percentages from their pictures. If the tube is 10 centimeters long and the water rises 2 centimeters inside the tube, the percentage of water inside the tube is (2 cm/10 cm = ⅕ = 20%).

ACTIVITY (4)	MATERIALS	
Who Can Make the Water Rise the Highest?	plastic tray	oil-based clay
	large plastic tube with cap	4 to 5 birthday candles
	matches	water
	safety goggles	

WHAT TO DO:

▼ Set up your materials as in the previous two activities.

HYPOTHESIZING	**How high can you make the water rise in your tube?**

To find out, you can try anything you wish (within reason).

HYPOTHESIZING	**What will happen, for example, if you use more candles, or put more water in the tray, or change the way you put the tube over the candles?**
APPLYING	*Try It!*

▼ Measure the amount of water that goes up the tube.

COMMUNICATING	**Write down the height of the water in the tube in centimeters.**
VERIFYING	**What percentage of the total tube is occupied by water?**

▼ Repeat your experiment several times.

VERIFYING	**Write down how high you were able to make the water rise in the tube.**
VERIFYING	**Write down the highest percentage of water in the tube you were able to obtain: _____ %**
SUPPORTING	**What reasons can you give for any difference you observed among the percentages?**

TEACHER BACKGROUND INFORMATION

As a small group activity, challenging each group to make the water rise the highest in their tube can be highly competitive and motivating. By placing the tube quickly over the candle(s) and by using an increasing number of candles, students should observe the water rising higher inside the tube (in some cases as high as 55% of the total volume of the tube). If all other variables are controlled, students should observe that as they increase the number of candles, the water level rises.

If you have provided your students with a discussion of the fact that 20% of the air is oxygen and only oxygen can be used up during the burning of the candles, then students should view any percentage of water in their tubes that is greater than 20% to be discrepant with their hypothesis that water is rising in the tube to replace the oxygen used up by the burning candle. However, most students will not associate the rising water with the increase in heat produced by the increased number of candles. Students should identify heat as a factor in the water rise *after* performing Activities 5 and 6. Unless students suggest heat as a factor, do *not* introduce this idea at this time.

ACTIVITY **5**

How Can You Make the Membrane Move?

MATERIALS

rubber membrane or piece of balloon (about 9 cm x 9 cm)

large plastic tube	candles
matches	oil-based clay
small rubber band	safety goggles

WHAT TO DO

▼ Place 2–3 candles together in the middle of a flat clay pancake.
▼ Remove the cap from the tube.

▼ Put the rubber membrane over the hole on one end of the tube.
▼ Wrap a rubber band tightly around the membrane and the tube.
▼ Light the candles.

HYPOTHESIZING   **What do you think will happen to the shape of the membrane when you put the tube *quickly* over the candles?**

▼ Put the tube *quickly* over the candles.
▼ Be sure that the tube makes a tight seal with the clay.

OBSERVING   **What did you observe?**
SUPPORTING   **What reasons can you give for your observations?**
HYPOTHESIZING   **What will happen when you repeat the experiment using the balloon?**
OBSERVING   **What did you observe?**
SUPPORTING   **What reasons can you give for your observations?**
COMPARING   **How were your observations with the balloon like your observations with the membrane?**

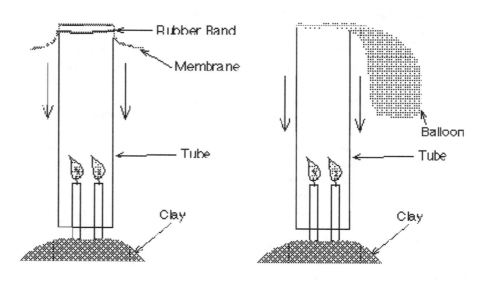

TEACHER BACKGROUND INFORMATION

Students should observe that the membrane will first rise and then be drawn into the tube. Their observations will depend on their ability to quickly place the tube over the candles and make a tight seal with the clay. If there are any openings under the tube to the outside air, they will not observe a movement in the membrane.

For most students, the rise in the membrane is the first observation in this Learning Cycle sequence that might lead them to hypothesize that the heating of the air inside the tube might increase the air pressure inside the tube and cause the air to expand. Like their observations with the rubber membrane, students should observe that the balloon first inflates while the candles are burning, and then is drawn inside the tube after the candles are extinguished. As before, results will depend on how students manipulate the materials.

MATERIALS

plastic tray	oil-based clay
large plastic tube with cap	birthday candles
water	matches
liquid detergent	safety goggles

WHAT TO DO

▼ Set the clay pancake in the bottom of the tray.

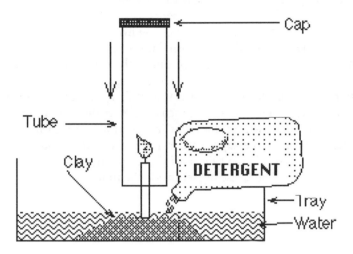

▼ Fill the plastic tray with water so that the clay pancake is covered.
▼ Set one or two candles in the middle of the clay pancake.
▼ Light the candles.
▼ Put the cap tightly on the tube.
▼ Add 5–10 drops of liquid detergent to the water around the base of the candles.
▼ Quickly, place the tube over the candles.

OBSERVING   **What *new* observations did you make?**

When you put the tube over the burning candles, you should observe bubbles forming.

IMPORTANT: This time you do *not* want a tight seal with the tube in the clay.

CATEGORIZING   **Were most of the soap bubbles *inside* or *outside* the tube?**
OBSERVING   **Where did the soap bubbles come from?**
SUPPORTING   **What reasons can you give for your observations of where the bubbles were found?**
CATEGORIZING   **Were the bubbles produced while the candles were burning or after they had gone out?**
PREDICTING   **What changes in air pressure might have taken place inside the tube that would help explain your observation of the soap bubbles?**

In addition to your observations of the bubbles, you should have observed the water rising up in the tube.

PREDICTING   **What changes in air pressure might have taken place inside the tube that would help explain your observation that water was rising inside the tube?**

SUPPORTING   **What reasons can you give to explain any changes in air pressure that might have occurred?**

TEACHER BACKGROUD INFORMATION

Students should observe soap bubbles forming on the *outside* of the tube. By asking them where the bubbles came from, guide them to conclude that as air was being forced out of the tube (while the candles were burning), bubbles were produced when the air came in contact with the soapy water. This escape of air occurred in earlier activities (2–4) but is much more noticeable when soap is added. Students might have observed the bubbles in earlier activities but dismissed them as not being important observations.

With your help, students should offer the hypothesis that the air inside the tube expands when heated, thus increasing the air pressure inside the tube. With no place to go, some of the air is forced out of the tube and is observed as soap bubbles. When the flame goes out, the remaining air inside the tube cools and contracts, resulting in a lowered air pressure. At this point the air pressure *outside* the tube (about 15 pounds per square inch) is greater than the air pressure inside the tube and pushes down on the water in the tray, causing water to enter the tube to replace the air that escaped earlier. The more candles you use (Activity 4), the hotter the air is inside the tube, and the more air is forced out of the tube. Therefore, the water should rise higher inside the tube.

ACTIVITY (7)

How Can You Now Explain the Mystery of the Rising Water?

MATERIALS

WHAT TO DO

Earlier, in Activity 2, you observed water rising inside the tube. You might have hypothesized that the water rose in the tube to replace the oxygen that was used up by the burning candles. Recall that 20 percent of the air is oxygen and *only* the oxygen in the air can be "used up" when the candles are burning. So the water should have risen inside the tube to occupy not more than 20 percent of the volume of the tube. However, in Activity 4, you made a puzzling discovery! You discovered that the water rose much higher than you expected. You observed that the more candles you used, the higher the water rose inside the tube (Activity 4). In Activity 5 you observed that the rubber membrane and balloon rose while the candles were burning and moved downward toward the inside of the tube *after* the candles went out.

PREDICTING   **What might have produced the higher pressure inside the tube that caused the rubber membrane and balloon to rise?**

In the last activity (6), you observed soap bubbles that formed mostly on the *outside* of the tube. When the air bubbles were pushed out from the inside of the tube, the air pressure inside the tube was higher than the air pressure outside the tube.

RELATING   **What could have caused the greater air pressure inside the tube?**

| RELATING | What might have caused the water to rise inside the tube *after* the candles went out? |

Think again about why the water rose in the tube with the burning candles.

COMPARING	What does the soap bubble activity (6) have in common with the rubber membrane and balloon activity (5) that might help explain why the water rose in the tube?
SUPPORTING	How does your observation—using more candles makes the water rise higher in the tube—help explain the rising of the water inside the tube?
INFERRING	From all of your observations and discussion, how can you now explain the mystery of why the water rose in the tube?

TEACHER BACKGROUND INFORMATION

At the end of this activity, your students should have been introduced to the concept, When air is heated it expands, and when cooled, it contracts. To enable students to discover this concept, you must play an active role in guiding them to make observations, compare observations from one activity to another, identify similarities among observations made, and draw inferences based on these observations and comparisons.

After you are comfortable that your students understand the discrepancy in Activity 4 between the expected 20% water rise and the observed greater-than-20% rise of water in the tube, you should encourage your students to identify similarities among Exploration Phase activities that will lead them to use *heat* to explain observations that suggest differences in air pressure. Students should identify similarities among the rising rubber membrane and balloon (5), the soap bubbles forming on the outside of the tube (6), and the increased volume of water in the tube due to the use of more candles (4). They should infer that these observations are caused by an increased pressure inside the tube resulting from an increase in temperature of the air inside the tube. When the source of heat (burning candles) is eliminated, the air pressure is reduced *inside* the tube and the air pressure *outside* the tube pushes down on the water (4, 6) or rubber membrane or balloon (5) causing the water or membrane or balloon to move into the tube.

Application Phase activities will serve as Exploration Phase activities for those students who do not as yet see the relationship between heat and the expansion and contraction of air in the Exploration Phase activities. Activity 9 (soda can activity), in particular, helps many students to change their tightly held initial hypothesis that the oxygen was used up to the more accurate heat hypothesis. This is because there is no fire or burning in the soda can activity—just heating air inside the can by means of a hotplate.

Teacher Demonstration

ACTIVITY **8**

The Mystery of the Egg and the Bottle

MATERIALS

glass milk bottle, or other glass or plastic bottle whose opening is comparable to that of a glass milk bottle

6-inch piece of paper with a width just smaller than the diameter of the bottle

2 hard-boiled eggs   matches

safety goggles

WHAT TO DO

▼ Select a hard-boiled egg that is slightly larger than the opening of a milk bottle.

▼ Remove the shell of the egg.

▼ Cut a 6-inch piece of paper with a width just smaller than the diameter of the bottle.

▼ Light the paper with a match and drop it into the milk bottle.

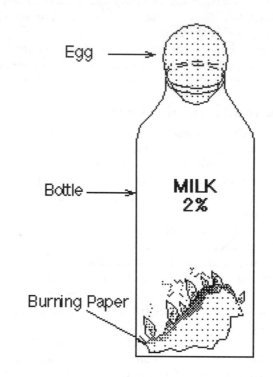

Egg →

Bottle →   MILK 2%

Burning Paper →

PREDICTING	**After you light one end of the piece of paper and drop it into the bottle, what will happen to the egg when you put it, pointed end down, into the mouth of the bottle?**
APPLYING	***Try it!***
OBSERVING	**What did you observe?**
INFERRING	**What conclusion can you give for your observation?**
COMPARING	**How is your observation of the egg like your observation of the rubber membrane and balloon in Activity 5?**
COMPARING	**How is your observation of the egg like your observation of the water as it rose inside the tube?**
APPLYING	**How could you use the egg demonstration to explain why the water rose in the tube?**

TEACHER BACKGROUND INFORMATION

If students have constructed an accurate concept that heated air expands and cooled air contracts, they should predict that the egg will be drawn into the bottle. Also, they should predict that the egg should *rise* slightly *before* it is drawn into the jar. As the air inside the jar is heated by the burning paper, the air expands. The egg is lifted by the expansion of air and some of the heated air is "pushed" out of the bottle. Because of the loss of air, the air pressure inside the bottle is lower when the air inside the jar begins to cool. With the lower pressure inside the bottle and the higher air pressure outside the bottle, the egg is "pushed" into the bottle. In comparing observations of the egg with the rising membrane and balloon, and the water that rises in the tube, students should identify the similar observations—the lifting of the egg, the rising membrane and balloon, and the bubbles outside the tube, all of which happen before the water rises in the tube—and relate them to the heat generated by the burning paper or candles.

Teacher Demonstration

How Can You Solve the Soda Can Mystery?

MATERIALS

large container, half-filled with cool water
2–3 empty 12 ounce soda cans
1 set of tongs
hot plate
safety goggles

WHAT TO DO

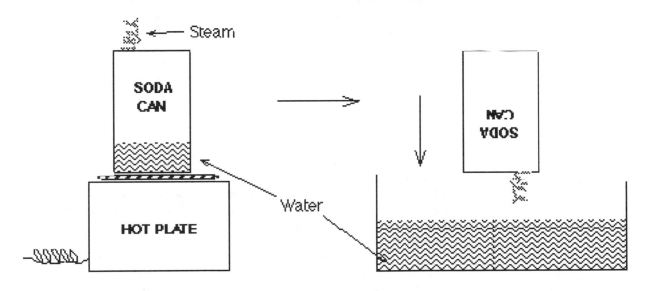

PREDICTING **What do you predict will happen to the soda can when we boil a small amount of water inside the can and then turn it upside down in a larger container of water?**

▼ Place about 5 milliliters (ml) of water into an empty 12 ounce soda can.
▼ Place the can on a hot plate. Heat until the water is boiling.
▼ When steam is pouring out of the opening in the can, use the tongs to quickly invert the can and place it immediately into a container of cool water.

OBSERVING **What changes in the can did you observe?**
INFERRING **What conclusion can you give for your observation?**
PREDICTING **How could the same results be obtained more quickly?**
PREDICTING **What would happen to the soda can if we repeated the experiment but this time did not put any water into the can?**

APPLYING *Try it!*

OBSERVING **What did you observe?**

COMPARING **How is your observation of the soda can like your observation of the egg-in-the-bottle activity in 8?**

CONTRASTING **How is it different form the egg-in-the-bottle activity?**

CONTRASTING **How is the soda can activity different from all the other activites you have done in this unit?**

RELATING **How can the observations of the soda can help explain why the water rises inside the tube with the burning candles?**

TEACHER BACKGROUND INFORMATION

Students should predict that when the soda can is heated, quickly inverted, and placed into a container of water, it will crumple and collapse. For best results, *quickly* invert the can and place the top of the can vertically into the container of cool water so that the opening in the can is quickly sealed with water. Students should predict that placing the can in colder water will produce a more dramatic crushing of the can as the colder water hastens the contraction of heated air remaining inside the soda can. Also, the water *inside* the can can be eliminated and only the air is heated. The steam produced by the boiling water is visible and students can more easily infer that air (and steam) is escaping from the can.

Students should be able to describe the changes occurring in the soda can step-by-step and how these changes relate to their observations. For example, students should state that heating the soda can causes the air inside to warm and expand. As the air expands, some escapes to the air outside the can. Thus, there are fewer air (and water) molecules left inside the can. When the can is taken off the heat source and quickly inverted into the cool water, the remaining air and water (and steam) contract, creating an area of lower pressure inside the can. The greater air pressure *outside* the can (about 15 pounds per square inch) pushes on the can, causing it to collapse. Comparisons of similar changes in pressure occurring in the other activities can be made.

In describing in a similar fashion changes occurring in the egg-in-the-bottle activity (8) and in activities related to the water rising in the tube, students should compare their descriptions and identify similarities among the activities—the heating of the air in the three containers, the heated air escaping from the three containers, and the changes occurring in the three containers.

Activity 9 (soda can activity), in particular, helps many students to change their tightly held initial hypothesis, that the oxygen is used up, to the more accurate heat hypothesis. This is largely because there is no fire or burning in the soda can activity—just the heating of air inside the can by means of a hotplate.

Following this activity, you might suggest that the egg-in-the-bottle activity (8) be revisited. When challenged to design an experiment to draw the egg inside the bottle *without using fire*, students might suggest placing a milk bottle or comparable glass or plastic bottle in a pan of hot water. After the air in the bottle has had an opportunity to warm, place the small end of a peeled hard-boiled egg in the opening of the bottle for a couple of minutes and then quickly place the bottle into the container of cool water. Students should observe that the egg is "pushed" into the bottle. If concentrated liquid detergent is thinly spread on the bottom third of the egg (or placed around the rim of the bottle opening) before the egg is placed in the bottle opening, students will observe soap bubbles as the heated air expands and escapes around the sides of the egg.

Circuits

▼

CONCEPT: *A circuit is a continuous pathway through which electricity flows.*

1 How many ways can you make a light-bulb light?

2 How can you make the bulb light with two wires?

3 What rule can you make to explain the lighting of the bulb?

4 Which bulbs do you predict will light?

5 How many bulbs can you light using one dry cell?

6 How does a bulb holder work?

7 How can you explain your bulb's behavior?

8 Where are the wires in your mystery box?

9 How can you make your bulb burn brighter?

10 How can you make a string of holiday lights?

11 How can you make a string of holiday lights a different way?

12 How can you explain the mystery bulb?

13 What's inside a bulb?

14 How can you make a lightbulb?

15 What materials will make the bulb light?

SUGGESTED LEARNING CYCLE SEQUENCE

Exploration Activities: Activities 1–2

Concept Introduction: Activity 3

Application Activities: Activities 4–15

INTRODUCTION

When asked to light a bulb given a dry cell (D-size, flashlight battery), a flashlight bulb, and a 10-inch piece of bare copper wire, many students (and adults) initially manipulate the three items as shown in the picture below.

This inaccurate picture of a circuit is described by Osborne and Freyberg (1985) and, from their research, represents a first level in the understanding of the concept of circuit for many children.

After performing Activities 1 and 2 in this Learning Cycle, students should be able to state that the bulb will light only when there is a closed pathway connecting two special places on the bulb and two special places on the battery. This pathway that allows the bulb to light is called a circuit.

Electric current flows only when there is a closed circuit. Electric current is made up of a flow of electric charges called electrons. In solid metals, like the copper wire used by students to make their circuit, the nuclei of the metal's atoms do not move easily from one place to another. In some metals, like copper, some electrons (free electrons) are not held tightly by their nuclei and can move easily from one atom to another. In a copper wire, for example, there is one free electron for each copper atom. It is estimated that when you switch on a 100-watt lightbulb in your home, approximately 6.25 million-million-million electrons enter and leave the filament each second (Schafer, 1992). This flow of electrons is called an electric current. A good conductor of electricity is a material that allows the electric current to flow through it easily.

The flow of electrical current through a wire can be compared to the flow of water through a pipe. The strength of water flowing through the pipe is determined by how much force or pressure is being applied at the end of the pipe. In an electrical circuit, the strength of the flow of electricity (electric current) is also determined by the amount of force or pressure applied to the wire in the circuit. In the water pipe system, the current of water moving through a particular cross section of pipe is measured in gallons per second. The pressure is measured in pounds per square inch. Electric current is measured in units called amperes and pressure is measured in volts. In both systems, the higher the pressure, the greater the current (Math 1981).

It should be noted that there are differences between the flow of electricity through a wire and the flow of water through a pipe. While water pipes are hollow, the wire is not. Although water flows downhill unless another force pushes it upward, electricity is not affected by gravity (Bakke and Rockcastle 1967).

The sequence of activities in this Learning Cycle represents but one of many different ways the concept of *circuit* could be presented to students. Indeed, as you gain experience with teaching of this concept, you may evolve your own sequence on the basis of your experiences and logic, as well as input provided by your students. Identify specific activities to be performed by all students. The remaining activities could be designated as optional and serve the needs of individual or small groups of students. While Activity 1 should be performed by each individual child, the remaining activities can be performed individually or in small groups.

LEARNING CYCLE STRATEGY

After gaining the necessary observations and experiences found in Activities 1 and 2 (Exploration Phase), the student has an introduction to the concept of *circuit* (Concept Introduction) in Activity 3. The remaining activities (4–15) form the Application Phase, which serves to reinforce, apply, extend, and expand the concept to new situations.

While all of the activities in the Application Phase of this Learning Cycle serve to expand or reinforce the concept of *circuit*, there are related subconcepts that could evolve into separate Learning Cycle topics. For example, a brief series of activities (12–14) focuses on how a bulb works and the role of a filament in the lighting of a bulb. Activity 12 could be viewed as an Exploration Phase activity in which a problem focus is established; Activity 13 introduces students to the structure and function of the functional parts of a bulb. Activity 14 could be viewed as an Application Phase activity that reinforces how a bulb works as well as resolves the problem focus introduced in Activity 12.

Activity 15 can serve as both an Application Phase activity that reinforces the concept of circuit, and as an initial Exploration Phase activity that provides experiences necessary for students to construct a concept of *conductor*. Thus, Activity 15 can be seen as a bridge from the concept of circuit to the concept of conductor.

The activities have been written as instructions and questions for your students, and each is accompanied by background information for you. As you work with students on the activities, feel free to make use of the drawings and charts included here. You may want to recreate some of the charts on an overhead transparency or on the blackboard so your students can refer to them.

SAFETY

While the activities found in this unit are safe, household electricity must be handled with care. Strongly emphasize to your students *not* to touch or play with electrical outlets or appliances with their fingers or wires. Any activities sent home with your students should have safety precautions written both to the students and their parents.

Dry cells and batteries are identified by the number of volts they produce. Those producing 1.5 volts should be used in this unit. These include the D cell (the common flashlight battery), the C cell, and the AA cell. Alkaline dry cells (D size) should be used, if available, for activities in this unit as they will last longer than non-alkaline batteries.

Students should not attach more than about 12 dry cells end to end (in series) in a circuit as they might receive a slight tingle or shock. Students should be told *not* to place a flashbulb or blasting cap, or similar devices in a circuit with their dry cell. Both can cause injury.

SOURCES OF MATERIALS

Some of the most common materials used in this unit are listed below with two of the many possible commercial sources.

MATERIAL	SOURCE
Bulbs: #48 Pink Bead	Delta Supply Company
#41 White Bead	P.O. Box M
Wire: Bare Copper	Nashua, New Hampshire 03061–6012
(#20) Thick	(603) 889–8899; 1–800–258–1302
Insulated Copper (#22)	
Nichrome (#26) Thick	Frey Scientific Company
Nichrome (#32) Thin	Elementary Science Catalog
Bulb Holders	905 Hickory Lane
	Mansfield, Ohio 44905
	1–800–225-FREY

*Note: #48 Pink Bead Bulbs are recommended as the only bulb type to be used in all activities except Activity 12.

#41 White Bead Bulbs are recommended to be used in Activity 12 only.

REFERENCES

Bakke, J., and Rockcastle, V.N. 1967. Cornell Science Leaflet: *Electric Circuit and Charges* 60 (4), 3–31.

Batteries and Bulbs: Introduction to Electricity and Magnetism, Teacher's Guide. 1986. Elementary Science Study Series. Nashua, NH: Delta Education.

Cash, T. 1989. *Electricity and Magnets.* New York: Warwick Press.

Cells, Lamps, and Switches. 1975. Science: A Process Approach II (Module 64). Nashua, NH: Delta Education, Inc.

Chapman, P. 1976. *The Young Scientist Book of Electricity.* London: Usborne Publishing Ltd.

Circuit Boards. 1975. Science: A Process Approach II (Module 61). Nashua, NH: Delta Education, Inc.

Circuits and Pathways: Teacher's Guide. 1990. Insights— Improving Urban Middle School Science. Newton, MA: Education Development Center.

Conductors and Nonconductors. 1975. Science: A Process Approach II. (Module 70). Nashua, NH: Delta Education, Inc.

Electric Circuits: Teacher's Guide. 1991. Science and Technology for Children. Washington, D.C.: National Science Resources Center.

Electrical Circuits: Teacher's Guide. 1988. A Delta Education Module. Nashua, NH: Delta Education, Inc.

Electricity. 1992. Operation Physics. Baton Rouge, LA: Louisiana State University.

Graf, R.F. 1964. *Safe and Simple Electrical Experiments.* New York: Dover Publications, Inc.

Gutnik, M.J. 1986. *Simple Electrical Devices.* New York: F. Watts.

Hansen, P. 1980. "Make a Quiz Board." *Science and Children* 17 (5): 36–37.

Iona, M. 1982. "Teaching Electricity." *Science and Children* 19 (5): 22–23.

Jennings, T. 1990. *Electricity.* New York: Gloucester Press.

The "Magic" of Electricity: A School Assembly Program. 1985. Great Explorations in Math & Science (GEMS). Berkeley, CA: Lawrence Hall of Science.

Magnetism and Electricity: Teacher's Guide. 1981. SAVI/SELPH. Berkeley, CA: Center for Multisensory Learning, Lawrence Hall of Science.

Markle, S. 1989. *Power Up: Experiments, Puzzles, and Games Exploring Electricity.* New York: Atheneum Publishing Co.

Marson, R. 1990. *Electricity: A Task Card Module.* Task Oriented Physical Science (TOPS). Canby, OR: TOPS Learning Systems.

Math, I. 1981. *Wires and Watts.* New York: Aladdin Books.

Osborne, R., and Freyberg, P. 1985. *Learning in Science.* Portsmouth, NH: Heinemann.

Schafer, L.E. 1992. *Taking Charge: An Introduction to Electricity.* Washington, D.C.: National Science Teachers Association.

Schwartz, M.L., and Schwartz, I.C. 1986. "From Batteries and Bulbs to High Tech." *Science and Children* 24 (1): 28–29.

Scott, J.M. 1981. *Electricity, Electronics, and You.* Portland, ME: J. Weston Walch.

Tipps, S., and Pisko, D. 1981. "'Light-on' learning." *Science and Children* 18 (4): 28–29.

Van Cleave, J. 1994. *Electricity.* New York: John Wiley & Sons, Inc.

Vogt, G. 1986. *Generating Electricity*. New York: F. Watts.

Whyman, K. 1989. *Sparks to Power Stations—Projects with Electricity*. New York: Gloucester Press.

Zubrowski, B. 1991. *Blinkers and Buzzers* (A Boston Children's Museum Activity Book). New York: William Morrow and Company, Inc.

ACTIVITY ①

How Many Ways Can You Make a Lightbulb Light?

MATERIALS

one dry cell (battery) D size, alkaline type if available

one 8-inch bare copper wire   1 flashlight bulb

WHAT TO DO

▼ Look at the flashlight bulb, 1 dry cell (flashlight battery), and copper wire on your table.

COMMUNICATING	**Draw a picture of how you think you can make the bulb light using these materials.**

▼ After you have drawn your picture, make your bulb light.

▼ If you try to light the bulb and the bulb does *not* light, your copper wire might become warm. This will wear out your dry cell more quickly.

▼ So try another way to light your bulb.

HYPOTHESIZING	**How many different ways can you get your bulb to light?**
COMMUNICATING	**Draw pictures of ways that you got the bulb to light.**
COMMUNICATING	**Draw pictures of ways that did not work for you.**

TEACHER BACKGROUND INFORMATION

To light the bulb, a connection must be made with the metal ends (top and bottom) of the dry cell and the side (brass) and bottom (silver) tip of the base of the bulb.

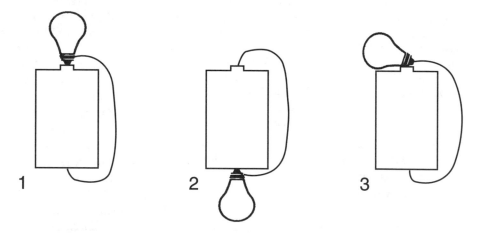

Notice that in diagrams 1, 2, and 3 above, these special places on the dry cell and bulb are being touched to form a circular pathway of metal touching metal.

Each student should be given his or her own dry cell, wire, and bulb for this initial activity. They should not be told how to light the bulb; that should be their own discovery. This will require patience on your part. Usually, after a few minutes one student will succeed in lighting the bulb. Other classmates will quickly observe his or her technique and be eager to succeed on their own. If, after 5–10 minutes, no success is met, a few helpful hints to an individual student might be necessary.

MATERIALS

one, dry cell D size   1 flashlight bulb
two 8-inch bare copper wires   cellophane tape

WHAT TO DO

▼ Using your materials, make the bulb light when it is *not* touching the dry cell.

COMMUNICATING	**Draw a picture to show how you were able to get the bulb to light.**
CATEGORIZING	**To light the bulb, what special places on the dry cell must be touched?**
CATEGORIZING	**What special places on the bulb must be touched for it to light?**

▼ Now try to light the bulb the same way but this time use just *one* wire.

COMMUNICATING	**Draw a picture showing where you think the wire should go to make the bulb light.**
VERIFYING	**Were you able to light the bulb this time?**
COMMUNICATING	**Using a crayon, draw a line on your first picture to show where you think the electricity is traveling.**
SUPPORTING	**What reasons can you give for your results?**

HINT: This time you will need two wires to light the bulb. You may work with a partner to light the bulb.

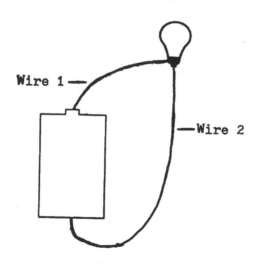

Wire 1 —

—Wire 2

TEACHER BACKGROUND INFORMATION

Students will discover that two wires are necessary for the bulb to light and that the wires must be connected as shown in the picture above. The bulb will light because all special places on the bulb and dry cell are touching metal. Although both special places on the bulb can be touched when using only one wire, the bulb in the circuit will not light because the electricity takes the easiest possible pathway and will travel through the single copper wire, bypassing the filament of the bulb. This is called a short circuit. If students have difficulty with this problem, ask them to recall from their earlier exploration (Activity 1) what special places must be touching. For this activity, students may work in groups of two or three to share wires and hands.

<table>
<tr><td>

ACTIVITY 3

What Rule Can You Make to Explain the Lighting of the Bulb?

</td><td>

MATERIALS

WHAT TO DO

CATEGORIZING	**From what you have observed, what special places on the bulb must be touched for it to light?**
CATEGORIZING	**From what you have observed, what special places on the dry cell must be touched for it to light?**
PREDICTING	**What else have you observed that must occur in order for the bulb to light?**
COMMUNICATING	**From what you have observed, make a rule about lighting the bulb.**

</td></tr>
</table>

TEACHER BACKGROUND INFORMATION

Following a discussion of student observations, the introduction of the concept of *circuit* (Concept Introduction) can be made. Students should be able to provide an operational definition of circuit—one that is based on the experiences gained from the manipulations required for them to light the bulb in Activities 1 and 2. Students should have observed the continuous (or closed) circular pathway of the dry cell, wire, and bulb and that all special places on the dry cell and bulb must be touching metal. An excellent discussion of preconceptions students have about the nature of an electrical circuit and strategies for helping students construct a scientifically accurate concept of a circuit is found in the book, *Learning in Science*, by Osborne and Freyberg (see References).

ACTIVITY 4

Which Bulbs Do You Predict Will Light?

MATERIALS

one dry cell D size	one flashlight bulb
two 8-inch bare copper wires	ditto sheets
pencil	

WHAT TO DO

Before you test each of the following nine circuits *predict* what will happen to the bulb in each circuit. (*Predicting*) Put your predictions in the blank spaces.

▼ Now test each of the nine circuits with your dry cell, bulb, and wire. (*Applying*)

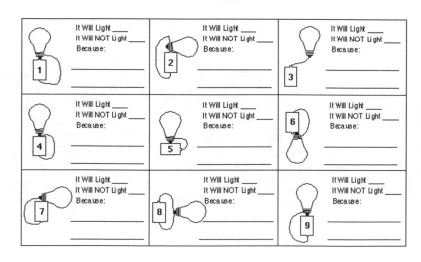

VERIFYING	**How many did you get correct?**
SUPPORTING	**What reasons can you give for any wrong predictions?**

▼ For each of the following eight pictures, draw in the wires needed to light the bulb.

▼ Use the *fewest* wires you can to light the bulb in each picture.

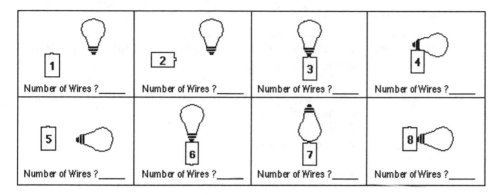

▼ Use your dry cell, bulb, and wire(s) to test each of the eight circuits you have made. (*Applying*)

CATEGORIZING	**In which of the eight circuits that you drew did the bulb not light?**
SUPPORTING	**What reasons can you give that the bulb did not light up in these circuits?**

TEACHER BACKGROUND INFORMATION

After students have manipulated materials, discussed their observations, and the concept of *circuit* has been introduced, Activities 4 and 5 can help to evaluate the students' understanding of circuit before they go on to activities that apply and extend the concept to new situations.

These pictures can be given to each student as a ditto sheet or individual 8½ x 11 cards can be made for the pictures. Using the cards, you can interact with individual students as you move from group to group. By probing and listening to their responses and to their subsequent testing with the materials, you can gain valuable insight into how well students have constructed a more accurate concept of circuit. Based on this informal and diagnostic evaluation, you must then decide what percentage of desirable responses is sufficient in order for individuals or the class as a whole to continue in the sequence of activities. In the first set of nine circuits, the following circuits will allow the bulb to light: 1, 6, 7, and 9. Desired responses for the second set of eight circuits are shown below.

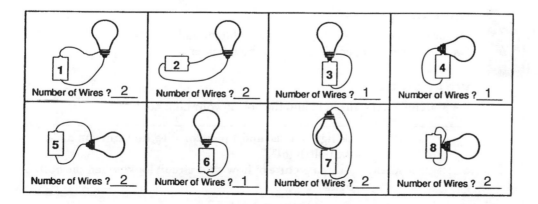

ACTIVITY **5**

How Many Bulbs Can You Light Using One Dry Cell?

MATERIALS

aluminum foil sheet (approximately 4 x 12)

two 8-inch bare copper wires   five or more flashlight bulbs
one dry cell D size

WHAT TO DO

HYPOTHESIZING	**Using 1 dry cell and 1 wire, how many bulbs can you light at one time?**
APPLYING	*Try it!*
HYPOTHESIZING	**Using 1 dry cell and 2 wires, how many bulbs can you light at one time?**
APPLYING	*Try it!*
OBSERVING	**What did you observe?**

▼ Now place the dry cell on a flat sheet of aluminum foil.

HYPOTHESIZING	**Using the foil, one dry cell, and one wire, how many bulbs do you think you can light at one time?**
APPLYING	*Try it!*
OBSERVING	**What did you observe?**
CONTRASTING	**What differences did you observe in the brightness of the bulb as you added bulbs to the circuit?**
SUPPORTING	**What reason can you give for your observations?**

TEACHER BACKGROUND INFORMATION

This activity can serve to help individualize instruction. While exploring with the materials, individual students and small groups will differ in the rate at which they pursue and complete specific tasks. To avoid potential management problems, students completing tasks at an accelerated pace can be given additional tasks to pursue. This activity is but one example of the many small challenges that can be used to enrich and extend the basic set of activities in this sequence and, at the same time, can occupy an individual student or small group while the remaining students continue to pursue the primary activity. Many of these kinds of activities will evolve from year to year from the questions and manipulations of the students. The teacher can develop and insert these activities into the instructional sequence of the unit.

ACTIVITY **6**

How Does a Bulb Holder Work?

MATERIALS

one dry cell D size   one flashlight bulb
two 8-inch bare copper wires   one bulb holder

WHAT TO DO

▼ Carefully screw the bulb into the hole in your bulb holder.

APPLYING	**Using 1 dry cell and 1 piece of wire, how can you make the bulb light?**
COMMUNICATING	**Draw a picture of how your circuit looks when the bulb lights.**

CATEGORIZING	**What special parts of the bulb holder helped to make the bulb light?**
RELATING	**What reasons can you give to explain how each of these parts helps to make the bulb light?**
CATEGORIZING	**What parts of your bulb were touching the bulb holder?**
CATEGORIZING	**Which of these parts on the bulb and the bulb holder are made of metal?**
COMMUNICATING	**Using a crayon, draw a line showing where you think the electricity travels in the circuit you drew.**
APPLYING	**Using 1 dry cell and *2 pieces of wire,* how can you make the bulb light?**

Your teacher will show you how to put the end of each wire into the 2 clips.

▼ Draw a picture of how your circuit looks. Your picture should include the bulb holder, dry cell, and 2 wires.

▼ Using a crayon, draw a line on your circuit showing where the electricity travels.(*Communicating*)

TEACHER BACKGROUND INFORMATION

The bulb holder shown was designed to allow students to more easily observe that the two special places on the bulb must be touching metal in order for the bulb to light. Thus, the concept of a circuit can be reinforced through this activity. You might use this opportunity to show students that by simply pressing down on either clip, the wire can be slipped into the hole. When pressure is released on the clip, the wire remains tightly clamped to the clip.

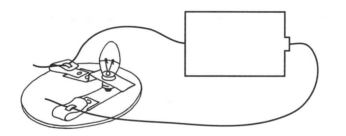

MATERIALS

one dry cell D size   one #48 flashlight bulb
two bare copper wires   one bulb holder

A C T I V I T Y **7**

How Can You Explain Your Bulb's Behavior?

WHAT TO DO

▼ Using your materials, make a circuit just like Circuit A.

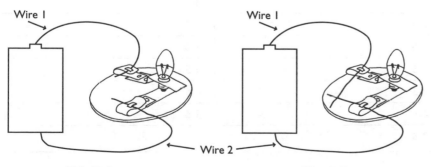

Circuit A   **Circuit B**

CATEGORIZING   **Does the bulb light?**

▼ Copy the diagrams of Circuit A and Circuit B.
▼ Using a crayon, draw a line on Circuit A showing where the electricity travels when wires 1 and 2 are *NOT* touching.

PREDICTING   **What do you predict will happen to the bulb in Circuit B when you touch the ends of wire 1 and wire 2?**
APPLYING   ***Try it!***
OBSERVING   **What did you observe?**
SUPPORTING   **What reason can you give for your observation?**

▼ Using a crayon, draw a line on Circuit B showing where the electricity travels when wires 1 and 2 are touching.

COMPARING   **How are your observations in this activity like your observation in activity 2?**

TEACHER BACKGROUND INFORMATION:

When wires 1 and 2 touch, the bulb will go out because the electricity travels through the thicker copper wire, bypassing (called a short circuit) the filament of the bulb. Students should be asked to compare their observations in this activity with their observations of the use of one wire in Activity 2.

ACTIVITY 8

Where Are the Wires In Your Mystery Box?

MATERIALS

one shoe box or similar small box
bare copper wire cut in 8-inch pieces

1 flashlight bulb   1 dry cell

WHAT TO DO

Look at the box your teacher has made. You should see six brass fasteners in the lid of the box. Under the lid there are copper wires that are connected to *some* of the brass fasteners. These wires are attached to other brass fasteners on the lid. Your task is to find out where the wires are placed in your box.

PAIRS	DID THE BULB LIGHT (YES OR NO)	PAIRS	DID THE BULB LIGHT (YES OR NO)
1-2		2-6	
1-3		3-4	
1-4		3-5	
1-5		3-6	
1-6		4-5	
2-3		4-6	
2-4		5-6	
2-5			

▼ Using 1 bulb, 1 wire, and 1 dry cell, invent a test that you can use to find out where the wires are connected without opening up the box. For example, how would you find out if there is a wire between brass fastener 1 and brass fastener 2? (*Applying*)

APPLYING   ***Try it!***

▼ Test all the possible pairs (listed in the chart above).
▼ Record your observations in a chart (like the one above). (*Communicating*)
▼ Based on your observations, draw a picture of how you think your box is wired. (*Communicating*)
▼ On the picture below, draw lines showing where you think *all* the wires are located. (*Communicating*)

> **NOTE:** Do *not* lift the lid of your box to see the wires!

> **HINT:** Connect your dry cell, bulb, and wire to brass fastener *1* and brass fastener *2*. Record if the bulb lights or does not light.

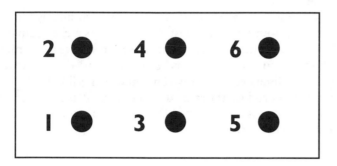

▼ After you talk about your picture with your teacher, open up your box.

VERIFYING	**Did your picture match how your wires were really connected in the box?**
INFERRING	**What conclusion can you give for any differences?**
COMMUNICATING	**What other different pictures can you draw that fit the observations you made on your box?**

▼ Draw these pictures on a piece of paper.
▼ Make a box of your own for your parents or friends to test.

TEACHER BACKGROUND INFORMATION

In discovering how their box is wired, this activity provides an excellent opportunity for students to *apply* their understanding of the concept of circuit learned in previous lessons. In addition, the lesson encourages students to observe, to record and classify data, and to infer patterns or circuits hidden from their view in the box. Thus, to evaluate students' ability to apply the concept of circuit, you should initially not show students how to use their materials in order to test each numbered pair on their box. Only when individuals or small groups have difficulty should you intervene with help. Initial student performance in manipulating the materials can help you evaluate student understanding of previous experiences.

Test boxes can be made by placing six brass fasteners in the lid of a small shoe box. Connect brass fasteners 1, 2, 4, and 6 with bare copper wires so that when each pair (1–2, 1–4, 1–6, 2–4, 2–6, 4–6) is connected with a bulb and dry cell, the bulb will light as a result of the complete circuit. Note, from the pictures below, that there are several ways the boxes can be wired to generate the above data. Some of these ways are shown below.

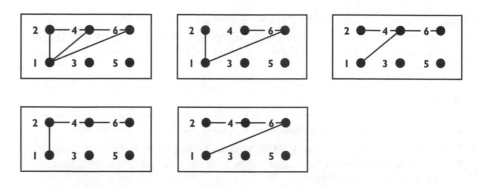

Brass fasteners 3 and 5 should not touch any of the copper wires. Before the students begin testing, the teacher might show them a model box and how it is wired to better communicate their task. It could be wired differently, e.g. wires placed from Fasteners 1–3–5.

Students can now test each pair of fasteners on their box by moving the dry cell, bulb, and wire from fastener to fastener. If used as a class activity, all boxes should be "wired" to produce the same data in order to have a common basis for class discussion. When observations have been recorded and pictures (inferences) drawn and discussed, students can remove the lid. That boxes can be wired differently but produce the same data allows students to infer a pattern of wiring for their box that is consistent with their data but not necessarily with the way their box was actually wired.

ACTIVITY **9**

How Can You Make Your Bulb Burn Brighter?

MATERIALS

one flashlight bulb   two 12-inch bare copper wires
2–5 dry cells   masking tape
empty toilet tube roll   flashlight from home

WHAT TO DO

▼ Using 1 bulb, 1 wire, and 1 dry cell, light the bulb.

HYPOTHESIZING	**How can you make your bulb burn brighter?**
APPLYING	*Try it!*
PREDICTING	**What will happen to the bulb each time you add one more dry cell to the circuit?**
APPLYING	*Try it!*
OBSERVING	**What did you observe?**

▼ Draw a picture using 3 dry cells to show a circuit that will light the bulb more brightly. Be sure to show how the wire is connected in your circuit.

RELATING	**How do the dry cells need to be touching each other for the bulb to burn brighter?**

▼ Using your materials, make a flashlight.
▼ Draw a picture of your flashlight. (*Communicating*)
▼ Look at a flashlight from home.

COMPARING	**How is it like the one you made?**
CONTRASTING	**How is it different?**

HYPOTHESIZING **How could you make the bulb in your flashlight burn brighter?**

HYPOTHESIZING **How could you make your flashlight easier to use?**

APPLYING *Try it!*

TEACHER BACKGROUND INFORMATION

Students can readily observe that when dry cells are connected in series (see below), the bulb burns more brightly. Connecting dry cells in series increases the voltage, or "pressure" behind the flow of electricity. Placing three 1.5 volt dry cells in series will produce approximately 4.5 volts of electricity.

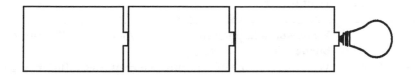

Allow one group to add enough dry cells to the circuit to burn out (break the filament of) one flashlight bulb. Discourage other groups from burning out their bulbs as it will greatly deplete your supply of bulbs. This activity serves as a prerequisite to many of the following activities. Empty toilet paper tubes and paper towel tubes make excellent "flashlights."

ACTIVITY **10**

How Can You Make a String of Holiday Lights?

MATERIALS

one dry cell D size
6 bulb holders

6 flashlight bulbs
ten 8-inch bare copper wires

WHAT TO DO

▼ Using your materials, make a circuit like the one in the picture below.

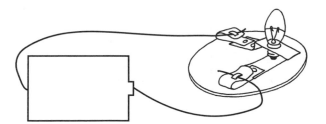

▼ Now add one more bulb in a bulb holder to the circuit. (*Communicating*)
▼ Do it in such a way that when one bulb is unscrewed (or burns out), the other bulb should *also* go out.

APPLYING *Try it!*

▼ Draw a picture of your new circuit containing 2 bulbs. (*Communicating*)
▼ Using a crayon, draw a line on the two circuits (A and B) to show where the electricity travels.
▼ Compare the observations you made of Circuit A and Circuit B.

CATEGORIZING **Which circuit had brighter bulbs, A or B?**

SUPPORTING	**Why did this happen?**
CONTRASTING	**In Circuit B, what difference did you observe in the brightness between the 2 bulbs?**
HYPOTHESIZING	**What reason can you give for this observation?**
PREDICTING	**When you unscrewed one bulb in Circuit B, why did the other bulb go out?**
PREDICTING	**What do you predict will happen to the brightness of the bulbs as more bulbs and bulb holders are added to Circuit B?**
APPLYING	***Try it!***
OBSERVING	**What did you observe?**

Suppose you had a string of streetlights in your neighborhood that were connected like Circuit B.

PREDICTING	**What would happen to the bulbs when one of the bulbs burned out?**
CATEGORIZING	**What is the name of a circuit that contains bulbs arranged like Circuit B?**
PREDICTING	**What would happen to the appliances in your home if they were arranged like the bulbs in Circuit B?**

TEACHER BACKGROUND INFORMATION

This activity should lead students to the introduction of the term *series circuit.* When bulbs are connected in series, all the electric current flows through each bulb when the circuit is closed. If identical bulbs are used, each bulb in the series circuit illustrated below will receive one-half the voltage from the dry cell. Thus, each bulb in the circuit will receive approximately 0.75 volts from a fresh 1.5 volt dry cell. Each bulb will appear, therefore, dimmer than just one bulb in the same circuit. If one bulb is disconnected from the circuit (or "burns out"), both bulbs will go out because there is no longer a complete pathway for the current—the circuit is broken. If students have difficulty building the circuit, try to diagnose their problem and guide them to success.

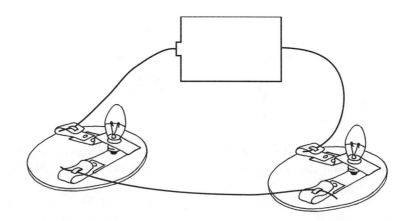

One group (perhaps the first to finish) could draw their circuit on a larger piece of paper for later display and reinforcement of the concept of *series circuit.* This lesson is often taught by initially providing students with a definition of a series circuit with an accompanying diagram. Students then are asked to use their materials to reproduce the circuit and verify its properties. Although this procedure will save time, it will probably not be so highly motivating for your students as it does not involve the resolution of a problem. Rather, it involves simply a verification of a given concept.

ACTIVITY 11

How Can You Make a String of Holiday Lights a Different Way?

MATERIALS

one dry cell
6 bulb holders
6 bulbs
10 wires

WHAT TO DO

- Using your materials, build a circuit with 2 bulbs in it. This time when one bulb is unscrewed (or "burns out"), the other bulb should *stay lit.*
- Both bulbs should be placed in the *same* circuit.

APPLYING **_Try it!_**

- Draw a picture of your circuit. (*Communicating*)
- Using a crayon, draw a line on your circuit showing where the electricity travels.

CONTRASTING **What differences do you observe in the brightness of the 2 bulbs in your circuit?**
SUPPORTING **What reasons can you give for your observations?**

- Unscrew one bulb so it goes out.

OBSERVING **What happens to the brightness of the other bulb?**
SUPPORTING **What reasons can you give for this observation?**
CATEGORIZING **What is the name of a circuit that contains bulbs arranged like your circuit above?**
PREDICTING **What do you predict will happen to the brightness of the bulbs as more bulbs are added to your circuit?**
APPLYING **_Try it!_**
OBSERVING **What did you observe?**

Suppose you had a string of neighborhood streetlights connected like your picture above.

PREDICTING **What would happen to the bulbs if one burned out?**
PREDICTING **What would happen to the appliances in your home if they were arranged like the bulbs in your circuit above?**

TEACHER BACKGROUND INFORMATION

This activity should lead students to the introduction of the term *parallel circuit.* When bulbs are connected in parallel, the electrical current branches off and more than one circuit is created. As a result, only part of the current goes through each bulb. Each bulb can, therefore, operate independently so that, if one bulb is disconnected (or burns out) from the circuit, other circuits are not broken and the bulb(s) in those circuits will continue to light. When identical bulbs are used, students should observe that the second bulb in the circuit burns as brightly as the first bulb. Each bulb receives the full voltage of the dry cell.

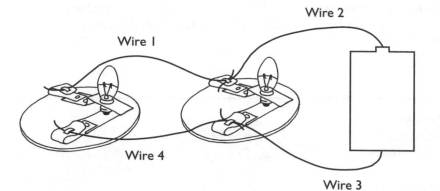

A good example of a parallel circuit is the double strand set of Christmas tree lights. All house circuits are wired in parallel so that all appliances and lights can be turned on and off separately without breaking the circuit.

ACTIVITY **12**

How Can You Explain the Mystery Bulb?

MATERIALS

one dry cell D size   two #48 flashlight bulbs
one #41 flashlight bulb   2 bulb holders
three 8-inch bare copper wires   hand lens (optional)

WHAT TO DO

▼ Using your materials, build a circuit like the one below. (*Communicating*)
▼ Using three wires, two bulb holders, two bulbs, and one dry cell, make one circuit with both bulbs burning equally bright in the circuit.

CATEGORIZING   **Are the bulbs in the circuit below connected in series or in parallel?**

Both bulbs should be burning with the same brightness.
▼ Now unscrew one bulb.
▼ Replace it with a bulb given to you by your teacher.

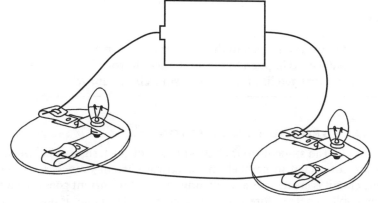

OBSERVING/COMPARING   **What changes did you observe in the brightness of**
AND CONTRASTING   **the two bulbs?**
SUPPORTING   **What reasons can you give for any differences you**
                         observed?

Look carefully at the inside of the two bulbs—the original bulb and the new bulb. Use a hand lens, if available.

CONTRASTING	**What differences did you observe between the 2 bulbs?**
COMMUNICATING	**What questions do you have about the new bulb and any differences between the two bulbs you observed?**

TEACHER BACKGROUND INFORMATION

If identical bulbs (pink bead, #48) are used initially, students should observe both bulbs lighting with equal brightness. However, when they are given a new bulb (possibly a white bead, #41), a discrepancy will arise. Students should observe that while the original bulb remains lit (and burns more brightly), the new bulb does not light. Students might hypothesize that this bulb is burned out. For these students, there is no discrepancy. They are satisfied with their explanation. Through probing, you will probably find that these students have little understanding of how a bulb works. If the bulb was burned out, the filament (and circuit) would be broken and the *other* (original) bulb also would not light. Activities 13 and 14 will help students better understand how a bulb works. When students test the new bulb by itself, however, they find that it *does* light—it is not "burned out." This creates for them a puzzling situation. To resolve the problem, they can observe differences between the original bulb and new bulb. They can observe differences in the color of porcelain beads inside each of the bulbs and, if they observe closely, differences in the filaments of the two bulbs.

Closure should not be reached at the end of this activity. To explain why the new bulb did not light in the circuit (and how the two bulbs are different), Activities 13 and 14 should be performed. Following Activity 14, students should infer that the thickness of the wire "filament" might explain the difference in behavior between the two bulbs.

ACTIVITY **13**

What's Inside a bulb?

MATERIALS

variety of good (working), clear, nonfrosted household bulbs
variety of burned-out, clear, nonfrosted household bulbs

WHAT TO DO

▼ Look carefully at the inside of your bulb.

OBSERVING	**What do you notice inside the bulb?**

▼ Carefully draw a picture of what you see. (*Communicating*)
▼ Using a crayon, draw a line on your picture showing how the electricity might travel through the bulb. (*Communicating*)

OBSERVING	**What part of the bulb glows when the bulb is lit?**
CATEGORIZING	**What do we call that part of the bulb?**
RELATING	**What happens when a bulb burns out?**

▼ Examine the burned-out bulbs that your teacher has for you.

CONTRASTING	**How are these bulbs different from the good (working) bulbs?**

TEACHER BACKGROUND INFORMATION

Students can observe the filament using clear household bulbs. You can carefully break frosted bulbs inside a paper sack. All glass should be removed from the base of the bulb.

ACTIVITY (14)

How Can You Make a Lightbulb?

MATERIALS

one 1-inch piece of #32 Nichrome wire
one 1-inch piece of #26 Nichrome wire

four new dry cells D size)	small ball of clay
two 10-inch bare copper wires	masking tape

WHAT TO DO

In the last activity (13), you identified the *filament* as the part of the bulb that glows when the bulb is lit. In this activity you are going to make a lightbulb that works! You will use a filament made out of Nichrome wire that will glow when your circuit is closed.

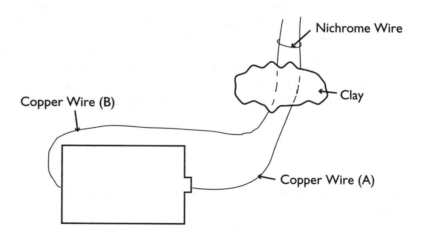

▼ Build the circuit with your materials.
▼ Place the ends of the two copper wires through a piece of clay shaped like a small pancake.

1. Use the clay to keep the copper wires from touching each other.
2. Place the ends of the 2 copper wires about 6 millimeters ($\frac{1}{4}$-inch) apart.
3. Wrap a 1-inch piece of thin (#32) Nichrome wire around the ends of each of two copper wires. This is the *filament* for your bulb.
4. Using the opposite ends of the two copper wires, put one dry cell into the circuit.

NOTE: There should be *only 1 strand* of Nichrome wire between the 2 copper wires.

OBSERVING	**What do you notice happens to the thin Nichrome wire filament when the circuit is completed?**
OBSERVING	**What do you notice happens to the thin Nichrome wire filament when more dry cells are added one at a time to the circuit?**
VERIFYING	**How many dry cells did it take to make the thin Nichrome wire glow?**

▼ Now replace the thin Nichrome wire filament with the thicker Nichrome wire filament.

VERIFYING	**How many dry cells did it take to get the thicker Nichrome wire to glow?**
CATEGORIZING	**Which filament glowed with the *smallest* number of dry cells?**
RELATING	**How can this activity help explain the differences you observed between the 2 bulbs in Activity 12?**

NOTE: Do *not* let the wire glow for more than 10 seconds or your dry cells will wear out.

TEACHER BACKGROUND INFORMATION:

Through this activity, students observe that the diameter of wire can affect the brightness of the bulb. Students should discover that the thin Nichrome wire (filament) will glow brightly using 1 or more fresh dry cells. Have students begin with one dry cell and use additional dry cells only as needed. The thicker Nichrome wire (filament) will become hot and usually will glow with the addition of one or more dry cells. The thin filament should be used first to gain motivation from initial success. Thin and thick(er) galvanized steel wire or course and fine steel wool can be substituted for the Nichrome wire. Try them first before you use them with your students.

During the experiment the two copper wires should not be touching. This will cause a short circuit and the electricity will bypass the Nichrome filament. The clay is used only to separate the copper wires. A thicker wire provides a broader pathway for the flow of electricity. A thin wire constricts the flow. In the effort to crowd through the narrow pathway in the thin Nichrome wire, much friction (resistance) is created and the wire becomes hot. If thin enough and when made of materials such as tungsten (used in many household bulbs) or Nichrome, it can also produce light in addition to heat.

From this activity, students can infer that differences in the two bulbs (pink and white bead) are due to differences in the thickness of the filaments. The pink bead might contain a thinner filament than the white bead bulb. Students can again look carefully at the filaments of the two bulbs and observe that these differences do indeed exist. This can serve to verify observations made in this experiment. It is important that in order for students to infer that the diameter of wire affects the ability of the filament to glow, all other variables, like length of the filament (distance between the two copper wires), number of dry cells, and the use of identical dry cells, must be carefully controlled. Indeed, formal attention to the process skill of *controlling variables* could serve as an important objective for this lesson.

ACTIVITY 15

What Materials Will Make the Bulb Light?

MATERIALS

box containing a variety of small objects, e.g. chalk, paper clip, penny, aluminum foil, clothespin, nail, wires of different materials—copper, aluminum, steel

three dry cells D size
1 bulb holder

1 flashlight bulb
three 8-inch bare copper wires

WHAT TO DO

▼ Using three wires, one bulb holder, one bulb, and one dry cell, build a circuit so the bulb will light. (*Communicating*)

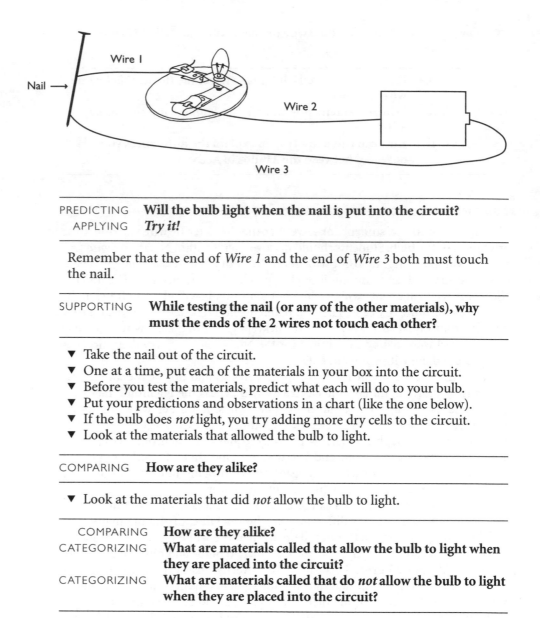

PREDICTING   **Will the bulb light when the nail is put into the circuit?**
APPLYING   ***Try it!***

Remember that the end of *Wire 1* and the end of *Wire 3* both must touch the nail.

SUPPORTING   **While testing the nail (or any of the other materials), why must the ends of the 2 wires not touch each other?**

▼ Take the nail out of the circuit.
▼ One at a time, put each of the materials in your box into the circuit.
▼ Before you test the materials, predict what each will do to your bulb.
▼ Put your predictions and observations in a chart (like the one below).
▼ If the bulb does *not* light, you try adding more dry cells to the circuit.
▼ Look at the materials that allowed the bulb to light.

COMPARING   **How are they alike?**

▼ Look at the materials that did *not* allow the bulb to light.

COMPARING   **How are they alike?**
CATEGORIZING   **What are materials called that allow the bulb to light when they are placed into the circuit?**
CATEGORIZING   **What are materials called that do *not* allow the bulb to light when they are placed into the circuit?**

THINGS TESTED	I PREDICT THE BULB WILL LIGHT/ WILL NOT LIGHT	I OBSERVED THAT THE BULB LIT/DIDN'T LIGHT
1		
2		
3		
4		
5		
6		

TEACHER BACKGROUND INFORMATION

In testing a large number of objects, students will observe, record, and categorize these objects into two groups based on whether the bulb lights or does not light. This strategy (inductive or guided discovery) should lead students to infer that when metal objects are placed into a circuit, the bulb will light. The introduction or invention of the terms *conductor* and *nonconductor* (insulator) should come at the end of the lesson, *after* the students have identified similarities among those objects that allowed the bulb to light. Activity 15 can be viewed as a bridge from the concept of circuit to the concept of conductor. In addition to reinforcing conductor by testing a wide variety of new objects, the concept can be expanded to include the identification of certain nonmetals that make the light bulb light (these nonmetals are conductors); for example, the graphite of a pencil and certain solutions—saltwater, baking soda solution, full-strength vinegar, diluted hydrochloric acid.

Density

> **CONCEPT:** *Objects and solutions differ from each other in their heaviness, or mass, per unit volume (density).*

1 The amazing aquarium (Teacher Demonstration)

2 What happens to different colors of food coloring in water?

3 What happens when food coloring is added to salt water?

4 How much does salt water weigh?

5 How can you make two layers in a vial using salt?

6 How can you make an egg float?

7 How can you explain your observations with food coloring, water, and salt?

8 Which solution is the heaviest; which is the lightest?

9 How can you make liquid layers in soda straws?

10 How do the solutions differ in heaviness?

11 How much does water weigh?

12 Find the density of a salt solution.

13 Can you put the densities on the graph?

14 Find the density of a rubber stopper.

15 The great root beer mystery (Teacher Demonstration)

16 What is the density of an egg?

17 Activity 1 revisited: What new ideas do you have?

SUGGESTED LEARNING CYCLE SEQUENCE

Exploration Activities:	Activities 1–6
Concept Introduction Activity:	Activity 7
Application Activities:	Activities 8–17

INTRODUCTION

Ideas for many of the activities in this sequence came from the Elementary Science Study (ESS) unit, *Colored Solutions*. The primary concept developed in this sequence is *density*, the idea that objects and solutions differ from each other in their heaviness, or mass, per unit volume. A dense object or liquid has more heaviness in a given space than a less dense material in that same space.

The first activities in the sequence (Activities 1–10) deal with density in a qualitative manner—without actually mathematically calculating the densities of the various solutions. Students develop the concepts that salt water is heavier than tap water and that more dense salt solutions can be made by increasing the concentration of salt. Activity 11 is an important activity in that it quantitatively defines the density of water as 1 gram per milliliter. The density of water serves as a basis for comparing the densities of other substances. For example, an object having a density of 3.0 g/ml is three times heavier than an equal volume of water. In the latter part of the sequence, students calculate the density of various objects such as rubber stoppers, eggs, and soda cans.

Temperature is another factor that affects the density of solutions. Hot water is less dense than cold water. There are a number of activities that could be identified and placed into this Learning Cycle sequence to develop this subconcept.

LEARNING CYCLE

In examining the sequence of activities within the topic of density, the following represent two different Learning Cycles that can be envisioned for this sequence of activities.

1. Students performing Activities 1–6 observe properties of food coloring, tap water and salt water (Exploration Phase). Students have made observations related to the concepts that salt water is heavier than tap water and that salt water can be made heavier by increasing the concentration of salt. With the introduction of these concepts (Concept Introduction) in Activity 7, Activities 8–17 represent activities that apply or extend these concepts to new situations (Application Phase).

2. Activities 1–11 provide experiences that help to develop an operational definition of density that is more quantitative. These activities could form the Exploration Phase. The formal introduction of the term density at the end of Activity 11 could be the Concept Introduction Phase. Activities 12–17 apply the concept to new situations (Application Phase).

SAFETY

Although the materials used in this sequence are safe, you should remind your students *not* to taste any liquid.

MATERIALS

The following materials needed in the teaching of the Learning Cycle sequence can be purchased from science supply companies such as Delta Education, P.O. Box M, Nashua, NH 03061–6012 (1–800–258–1302): plastic aquarium, 250 ml flasks, medicine droppers, 30 ml medicine cups, plastic dropper bottles, plastic vials, rubber stoppers, equal-arm balance, cube-o-gram weights.

The activities have been written as instructions and questions for your students, and each is accompanied by background information for you. As you work with students on the activities, feel free to make use of the drawings and charts included here. You may want to recreate some of the charts on an overhead transparency or on the blackboard so your students can refer to them.

REFERENCES

Bernstein, L., Schachter, M., Winkler, A., and Wolfe, S. 1986. *Concepts and Challenges in Physical Science*, Second Ed. Newton, MA: Allyn and Bacon, Inc.

Colored Solutions: Teacher's Guide. 1986. Elementary Science Study Series. Nashua, NH: Delta Education.

Density. 1975. Science: A Process Approach II (Module 103). Nashua, NH: Delta Education, Inc.

Detwiler, B. 1991. "Root Beer Float." *CommuniKAPS: Kentucky Science Teachers Association Newsletter*, ed. R. Fiel, Morehead State University, Morehead, KY 40351. 42, Spring.

Discovering Density: Teacher's Guide. 1988. Great Explorations in Math & Science (GEMS). Berkeley, CA: Lawrence Hall of Science.

Floaters and Sinkers: Teacher's Guide. 1987. Project AIMS. Fresno, CA: AIMS Education Foundation.

Goldberg, V., Williams, S., and Hite, S. 1990. "Edible Density." *Science and Children* 27 (5): 20–22.

Halpin, M.J., and Swab, J.C. 1990. "It's the Real Thing—The Scientific Method." *Science and Children* 27 (7): 30–31.

Kitchen Interactions: Teacher's Guide. 1981. SAVI/SELPH. Berkeley, CA: Center for Multisensory Learning, Lawrence Hall of Science.

Liquids: Teacher's Guide. 1991. Insights—Improving Urban Middle School Science. Newton, MA: Education Development Center, Inc.

Marson, R. 1978. *Floating and Sinking: A Task Card Module*. Task Oriented Physical Science (TOPS). Canby, OR: TOPS Learning Systems.

McGinnis, J.R., and Padilla, M.J. 1991. "The Great Hydrometer Construction Contest." *The Science Teacher* 58 (4): 20–25.

Nesin, G., and Barrow, L.H. 1984. "Density in Liquids." *Science and Children* 21 (7): 28–30.

Sarguis, M. 1994. "Density Batons." *Science and Children* 32 (1): 34–36.

Scheckel, L. 1993. "How to Make Density Float." *Science and Children* 31 (3): 30–33.

Sink or Float. 1988. A Delta Science Module. Nashua, NH: Delta Education, Inc.

Zielinski, E.J., and Sarachine, D.M. 1990. "Creativity and Criticism." *The Science Teacher* 57 (8): 18–20.

Teacher Demonstration

ACTIVITY 1
The Amazing Aquarium

MATERIALS

two corked 250 ml flasks, one completely filled with a blue liquid and one completely filled with a red liquid
1 aquarium filled to a water level exceeding the height of the flasks

WHAT TO DO

▼ Fill an Aquarium ¾ full of water.

▼ Have a student place the flask containing the blue liquid on the bottom of the filled aquarium.

▼ Have the student very slowly remove the cork from the flask and lift the cork slowly out of the aquarium.

▼ Have the student hold the flask in place on the bottom of the aquarium.

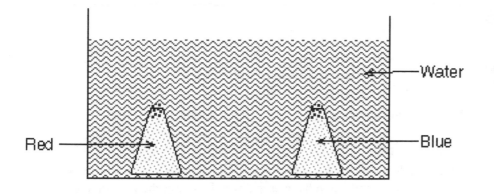

OBSERVING
What did you observe happening to the blue liquid inside the flask when the cork was removed?

▼ Using a second student, repeat the procedure for the flask containing the red liquid.

OBSERVING
What did you observe happening to the red liquid inside the flask when the cork was removed?

HYPOTHESIZING
What reasons can you give for your observations?

HYPOTHESIZING
What might the blue-colored liquid be made of?

HYPOTHESIZING
What might the red-colored liquid be made of?

HYPOTHESIZING
What might the clear liquid in the aquarium be made of?

TEACHER BACKGROUND INFORMATION

The purpose of the demonstration is to motivate students by using a puzzling situation (discrepant event) and to provide a problem focus for the activities that follow. One solution (blue) should be heavier than the water in the aquarium. This solution could be prepared by adding blue food coloring and salt (or sugar) to tap water to make a concentrated blue solution. The second flask (red solution) should be lighter than the water in the aquarium. This solution could be prepared by adding red food coloring and rubbing alcohol to tap water to make a dark red solution. If rubbing alcohol is used, the flask should contain about one-third alcohol and two-thirds water. By preparing the solutions in the above manner, the blue solution will remain in the flask while the red solution will rise to the top of the aquarium.

Fill both flasks to the very top so no air bubbles will exist when the corks are opened under water. As the flask containing the red alcohol solution is lighter than the surrounding aquarium water, you will need to physically hold the flask on the bottom of the aquarium. Otherwise, it will float up to the top. Following the demonstration, students should be encouraged to hypothesize how the solutions are different. However, closure should *not* be reached. Be ready to tip the blue flask over on its side. Students will observe that the blue solution "pours" out of the flask forming a layer on the bottom of the aquarium. Thus, if done carefully, students should observe a blue layer on the bottom, a clear layer in the middle, and a red layer on the surface of the aquarium. Ask students to predict how long they think the layers will remain distinct. In doing so, they might well be testing an hypothesis, so they have to explain their observations.

ACTIVITY ②

What Happens to Different Colors of Food Coloring in Water?

MATERIALS

one vial or baby food jar filled with water for rinsing medicine dropper
red, green, and blue food coloring
three vials or baby food jars half-filled with water
one container of clean water for refilling the vials

three medicine droppers   one dump bucket

WHAT TO DO:

▼ Carefully, place one drop of *red* food coloring into a vial or baby food jar. You might tilt the vial and roll the drop down the side of the vial into the water.

OBSERVING	**What did you observe happening to the drop of red food coloring when added to the water?**
SUPPORTING	**What reasons can you give for your observations?**

▼ Repeat the procedure using *blue* food coloring, then again using *green*.

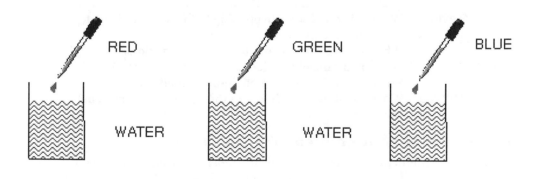

OBSERVING	**What did you notice happening to the blue food coloring when added to the water?**
OBSERVING	**What did you notice happening to the green food coloring when added to the water?**
COMPARING	**How were your observations of the three colors alike?**
CONTRASTING	**How were they different?**
CONTRASTING	**Explain any differences you observed.**
COMPARING AND CONTRASTING	**How do your observations in this activity relate to your observations in Activity 1?**
INFERRING	**In what ways do your observations of the different colors of food coloring help explain your observations of the liquids in the two flasks in Activity 1?**
SUPPORTING	**What reasons can you give for your answer?**

TEACHER BACKGROUND INFORMATION

This is an important activity in that students should observe little, if any, differences in heaviness among the three colors of food coloring. As dilute food coloring and water have roughly the same heaviness (density), students should observe no differences in how certain colors sink or float when placed in the water. Therefore, students should infer that the observations in Activity 1 (teacher demonstration) cannot be explained by differences in the heaviness of red and blue food coloring.

This activity provides a good opportunity for you to emphasize controlling variables when comparing one color to another. After the students have manipulated the materials and discussed their observations, each student should agree that the three colors acted similarly in the water. Any variation in the reaction of the colors is due to the methods and techniques the students utilized—not due to any differences in heaviness among the three colors of food coloring.

ACTIVITY ③

What Happens When Food Coloring Is Added to Salt Water?

MATERIALS

three vials or small baby food jars
blue, red, or green food coloring

medicine dropper	kosher salt or regular salt
spoon	water

WHAT TO DO

HYPOTHESIZING	**What differences do you think you will observe between food coloring added to water and food coloring added to salt water?**

▼ Set up the 3 jars as you see below.
▼ Add salt to the last 2 jars (B,C) as shown.
▼ Stir until the salt disappears in each jar.
The salt is *dissolved* in the water. A mixture of salt and water is called a *solution*. *Solutions* are made when substances dissolve in other substances.
▼ Carefully add *one* drop of food coloring to the solution in each jar.
▼ Remember to add the food coloring the *same* way to each jar.

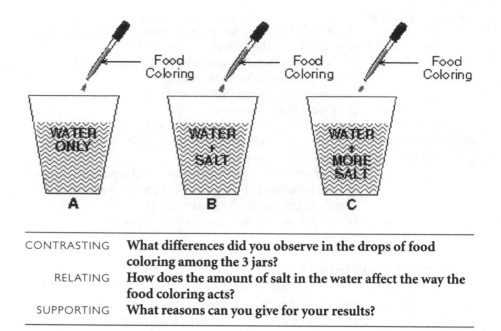

CONTRASTING	What differences did you observe in the drops of food coloring among the 3 jars?
RELATING	How does the amount of salt in the water affect the way the food coloring acts?
SUPPORTING	What reasons can you give for your results?

TEACHER BACKGROUND INFORMATION

Salt water is heavier (more dense) than water. Increasing the concentration of salt increases the heaviness (density) of the solution. Kosher salt is preferred as it dissolves rapidly and completely. The food coloring will diffuse in the tap water; however, it will float on top of the salt solution. As more salt is added to the water, students should observe a greater tendency for the drop of food coloring to float on the surface of the salt water. They might suggest that the addition of an increasing amount of salt results in a heavier (more dense) solution and the lighter drop of food coloring floats on the surface.

ACTIVITY **4**

How Much Does Salt Water Weigh?

MATERIALS

graduated plastic medicine cup   salt
gram masses (weights)   water
balance

WHAT TO DO

Anything that has weight and takes up space is called *matter*. Almost everything you see around you is matter. Matter is found in three forms—solids, liquids, and gases. Liquids, like the ones we will be studying in this unit, have definite volumes. The *volume* of liquids is often measured in liters and milliliters. There are 1000 milliliters in one liter. *Mass* is the actual amount of matter in a certain amount of a solid, liquid, or gas.

The *gram* is a unit of mass. The *weight* of an object depends on the pull of gravity on it. Objects weigh less on the moon than on the earth. The weight of an object changes when gravity changes, but the mass stays the same. When we measure solids and liquids in this unit, the mass of the object will be the same as the weight of the object.

▼ Place an empty cup on one side of the balance.

| MEASURING | What is the mass (weight) of the empty cup? |

▼ Add 15 milliliters of water to the cup.
▼ Weigh the cup on the balance.

MEASURING **What is the mass (weight) of the cup of water?**
MEASURING **What is the mass (weight) of the water itself?**

▼ Measure 10 grams of salt using a balance.
▼ Add the 10 grams of salt to the 15 ml cup of water.
▼ Stir until all the salt dissolves.

PREDICTING **What do you predict will be the mass (weight) of the salt water solution?**

▼ Weigh the salt water solution and record the weight in grams. (*Verifying*)

VERIFYING **What is the mass (weight) of the salt water solution?**
CATEGORIZING **From your observations, which is heavier, 15 ml of water or 15 ml of your salt water solution?**
RELATING **How do your observations in this activity help explain why the food coloring floated on top of the salt water in the last activity (3)?**

TEACHER BACKGROUND INFORMATION

Although the salt dissolves in water and disappears, it does add weight to the solution. As a result, salt water is heavier (more dense) than tap water. Students should observe that the solution will weigh approximately 25 grams plus the mass of the cup (10 grams of salt plus 15 grams of water). Fifteen milliliters of water weighs 15 grams (see Activity 11).

ACTIVITY 5

How Can You Make Two Layers in Your Vial by the Use of Salt?

MATERIALS

four vials or baby food jars   food coloring
medicine dropper   spoon
salt   water

WHAT TO DO

▼ Add salt to water in a vial to make a salt water solution. You may add as much salt as you like.
▼ Add food coloring to plain water in another vial.

APPLYING **Using your past observations with salt, water, and food coloring, how can you create a 2-layer solution in a third vial using the two solutions you created already?**

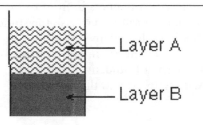
Layer A
Layer B

▼ Describe your investigation. (*Communicating*)

COMMUNICATING	How did you make layer A?
COMMUNICATING	How did you make layer B?
COMMUNICATING	How did you place layer A on top of layer B?
PREDICTING	What would happen if you tried to put layer B *on top of* layer A?
APPLYING	*Try it!*
OBSERVING	What did you observe?
SUPPORTING	What reasons can you give for your observations?
APPLYING	Now that you have put two layers in your vial, see how many layers you can make in your vial!
OBSERVING	How many different layers do you observe?

TEACHER BACKGROUND INFORMATION

Salt water is heavier than tap water. Be sure that students understand that food coloring does *not* affect the weight of the solution (see Activity 2). Be sure there is enough contrast in the colors for the students to observe the layers.

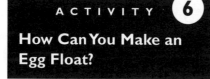

ACTIVITY **6**

How Can You Make an Egg Float?

MATERIALS

large glass or clear plastic container

fresh egg   salt
water

WHAT TO DO

▼ Fill the container half-full of water.

PREDICTING	When you place an egg in the water, do you think the egg will sink or float?
APPLYING	*Try it!*
OBSERVING	What did you observe?
RELATING	Using what you have learned so far, how can you make the egg float?
COMMUNICATING	Describe your experiment.
COMMUNICATING	How did you make your egg float?
COMMUNICATING	What explanation can you give for the floating of the egg in the water?

TEACHER BACKGROUND INFORMATION

Increasing the salt concentration of a solution allows objects to float more easily. This activity can also be used as a teacher demonstration or discrepant event. Place two unlabeled, identical containers in front of the class (one container of tap water and one container of salt water). Ask the students to predict whether the egg will float or sink in each container. Place one egg in each container and ask the students to explain why the egg in one container sinks and the egg in the second container floats. Then ask students how they can make the egg float and allow them to try it. Activity 16 extends this activity.

ACTIVITY **7**

**How Can You Explain
Your Observations with
Food Coloring, Water,
and Salt?**

MATERIALS

WHAT TO DO

In Activities 1–6 you discovered how food coloring, plain water, and salt affected the heaviness of solutions.

CONTRASTING	**From your observations, what differences in heaviness exist among the different food colorings you used?**
RELATING	**From your observations, how did the amount of salt in a solution affect its heaviness?**
INFERRING	**From what you have learned so far in activities 1–6, how could you make the heaviest possible solution?**
PREDICTING	**How could you make 5 different solutions of which each has its own heaviness?**

TEACHER BACKGROUND INFORMATION

This activity could be used to pull together observations your students have made in Activities 1–6. At the end of a discussion of their observations, students should conclude that increasing the concentration of salt in a solution will increase the heaviness (density) of the solution. Following the introduction of this concept, students can investigate a number of new problems that apply and extend these concepts to new situations. You might not want to arrive at closure on Activity 1 at this time. Activity 17 serves this purpose.

ACTIVITY **8**

**Which Solution Is the
Heaviest? Which Is the
Lightest?**

MATERIALS

four teacher-made solutions—green, clear, red, blue

three medicine droppers   salt
rubbing alcohol   5–6 vials

WHAT TO DO

Four mystery solutions—green, clear, blue, and red—have been prepared for you. Your problem is to arrange the four solutions in the correct order—from lightest to heaviest. Experiment using any of the materials listed above to discover how to order the four solutions from lightest to heaviest.

ORDERING	**How did you solve the problem and get the order of the four solutions?**

▼ From your observations, record your rank order. (*Ordering*)

SUPPORTING	**How did you determine the differences in heaviness you observed among the four solutions?**

PREDICTING   **How might your teacher have made the four solutions?**
HYPOTHESIZING   **Where do you think rubbing alcohol would go in your
4-layer heaviness chart?**

▼ Using any of your materials, find where alcohol fits in your 4-layer order.

OBSERVING   **What did you observe?**

▼ List the four colored solutions and the alcohol in what you think is the
correct order. (*Ordering/Communicating*)
▼ When you have completed this activity, begin Activity 9 to find out if your
order is correct.

TEACHER BACKGROUND INFORMATION

The higher the salt concentration, the greater the heaviness (density) of the solution. The order of the 4 solutions and their preparation:

Lightest: *Blue*—1 quart water + blue food coloring
Clear—1 quart water + 1/3 cup kosher salt
Red—1 quart water + 2/3 cup kosher salt + red food coloring
Heaviest: *Green*—1 quart water + 1 cup kosher salt + green food coloring

Note that Activity 8 is less structured and encourages students to devise their
own procedures. As a result, a variety of methods will be attempted within a class.
You can always provide more structured help to individual students or groups
who are floundering. Given previous experiences, students should be able to create their own procedures with minimum difficulty. Students could, for example,
add drops of one color to a vial of another color and observe whether the drops
sink or float in the solution. By testing a number of pairs, the order could be determined. Students might attempt to make layers of different colors within a single vial. Students should complete Activity 9 before they are given the correct
order (Blue, Clear, Red, Green). Activity 9 will verify their order. Sugar or table
salt can substitute for kosher salt.

ACTIVITY **9**

**How Can You Make
Liquid Layers in a Soda
Straw?**

MATERIALS

four teacher-made solutions made in Activity 8
three to four clear, plastic soda straws

rubbing alcohol   five empty vials or jars

WHAT TO DO

▼ Place 5 vials or jars on your table.
▼ Fill each vial ¾-full with one of the five solutions from Activity 8—green,
red, clear, blue, and alcohol.
▼ Select two of the solutions.
▼ Based on your observations in Activity 8, predict which of the two solutions
is the heaviest. (*Predicting*)
▼ Follow the directions below and make a two-layer sandwich in your soda
straw.
▼ When you have successfully made the two-layer sandwich, try to make
two-layer sandwiches using other solutions.
▼ Record your observations in a chart (like the one below). (*Communicating*)

1. Dip the straw about ¼-inch into the liquid you want on the top of your sandwich.

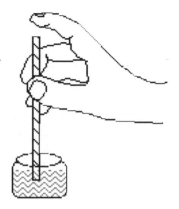

CATEGORIZING   **Will this liquid be the heavier or the lighter of the two liquids?**

▼ Keep the top of the straw *open*.

SUPPORTING   **What is the basis for your answer?**

---

2. Place your finger over the top of the straw and remove the straw from the liquid. A ¼-inch layer of liquid will remain in the straw.

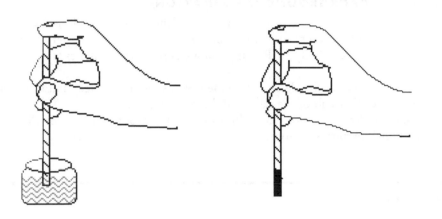

3. Keep your finger over the top of the straw and lower the straw about ¾-inch into the second solution of your choice.
   Release your finger and some of this solution will push the first layer up higher in the straw.
4. Put your finger over the top of the straw and remove it from the solution. If you have chosen the correct order, you will have a two-layer sandwich.

▼ When you have successfully made a two-layer sandwich, try to make two-layer sandwiches using other combinations of the four solutions.
▼ Record your observations in a chart (like the one below). (*Communicating*)

CHART FOR 2-LAYER SANDWICH							
Top Layer							
Bottom Layer							

▼ Using the above procedure, make a 4-layer sandwich in your straw with *each* of the four colored solutions making a layer in the straw.(*Applying*)
▼ First, make a prediction of what you think your sandwich will look like. (*Predicting*)
▼ Put your prediction in a chart (like the one below).
▼ After you actually made your soda straw sandwich, enter your observations into the chart.

OBSERVING   **What was the first colored solution you placed in the straw?**
SUPPORTING   **Why did you place it first in the straw?**
OBSERVING   **What was the last colored solution you placed in the straw?**
SUPPORTING   **Why did you place it last in the straw?**

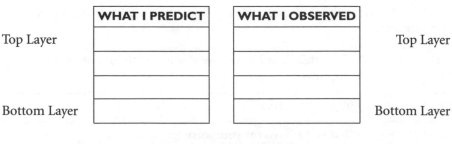

	WHAT I PREDICT	WHAT I OBSERVED	
Top Layer			Top Layer
Bottom Layer			Bottom Layer

INFERRING   **Based on your work, why do you think the four colored layers in your straw do *not* mix together?**

_____

TEACHER BACKGROUND INFORMATION

This activity should be used to verify the order of the mystery solutions discovered in Activity 8. At some point students should be told how the four mystery solutions were prepared (see Activity 8). Two appropriate enrichment activities are:

1. Have one half of the class prepare their own series of mystery solutions and have the other half of the class find the correct heaviness order.
2. Have students prepare new solutions that fit in-between two of the four original mystery solutions.

ACTIVITY 10

How Do the Solutions Differ in Heaviness?

MATERIALS

6 graduated plastic medicine cups (identical size)
25 ml graduated cylinder (if available)
4 mystery solutions (see Activity 8)

equal-arm balance   4 medicine droppers
rubbing alcohol

WHAT TO DO

▼ Weigh the empty cups on the balance and find six cups each having the same mass.
▼ Fill each cup with *exactly* 25 milliliters (ml) of each of the four different solutions (green, blue, clear, and red) that you used in Activities 8 and 9.
▼ Fill the fifth cup with *exactly* 25 milliliters (ml) of rubbing alcohol.
▼ Using all five solutions, select eight sets (pairs) of solutions. For example, take the cup of *blue* solution and the cup of *green* solution.

PREDICTING   **Which solutions, the blue or the green, will be the heaviest?**

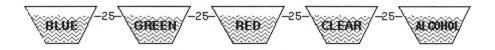

▼ Place the cups on the balance and observe any differences in mass (weight). (*Verifying*)
▼ Repeat for each of the other seven sets (pairs).

INFERRING   **Explain any differences you observed between your predictions and your observations.**

TEACHER BACKGROUND INFORMATION

Different solutions can have different densities. If the balances are sensitive enough, differences between any two of the solutions should be observed. The largest source of error will be in measuring the same volume of liquid in each cup. By having students line their cups up next to each other, these differences in volume will be observed and corrected before weighing. To reduce this source of error, students can pour 25 ml of each solution into separate 25 ml graduated cylinders. Having obtained a more precisely measured volume, they can then pour each solution into a medicine cup. Following this activity, students could prepare new mystery solutions to compare and weigh.

ACTIVITY **11**

How Much Does Water Weigh?

MATERIALS

blue solution (tap water and blue food coloring from Activity 8)
metric or standardized weights (paper clips, nickels, etc.)

30 ml graduated medicine cup   medicine dropper
equal-arm balance   cube-o-gram weights

WHAT TO DO

▼ Place an empty medicine cup on one side of the balance.

OBSERVING   **What do you observe is the mass (weight) in grams of the medicine cup?**

▼ Fill the medicine cup with exactly 25 ml of the blue solution.
▼ Carefully put it on one side of the balance.

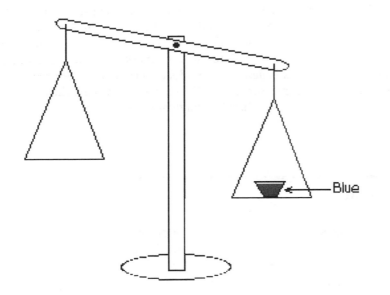

PREDICTING   **What do you predict will be the mass in grams of the 25 ml of the blue solution?**

▼ Add the mass weights to the other side of the balance until it is balanced.

VERIFYING   **How many grams did it take to balance the cup and the solution?**

Record the following information:

Number of grams to balance the cup and the solution.
Mass (weight) of the empty cup.
Mass (weight) of the empty cup plus the 25 ml of water.
Mass (weight) of the 25 ml of water.
Mass (weight) of 1 ml of water.

From your measurements, what is the mass of one milliliter (ml) of water?

DISCUSSION: Density is a way to describe the heaviness of something. It is the mass (in grams) per unit volume (in milliliters).

Formula: $\dfrac{\text{Mass (grams)}}{\text{Volume (milliliters)}} = \text{Density}$

VERIFYING   **Using the same formula, what is the density of water?**

In Activities 8 and 9, you found out which solutions were heavier and which were lighter.

▼ Using what you know about the density of water, find the density of the other liquids used in Activity 8. (*Applying*)

COMPARING AND
CONTRASTING
CATEGORIZING
How does the density of each of the solutions compare with the density of water?
Will the solutions that have a density greater than the density of water sink or float when carefully placed in plain tap water?

▼ Find the densities of other liquids such as oil and vinegar. (*Applying*)

TEACHER BACKGROUND INFORMATION

Density can be described as mass per unit volume (D = mass/volume; D = grams/milliliter). Students should observe that 25 ml of water weighs about 25 grams. From this observation, students can calculate the density of water (25 g/25 ml = 1.0 g/ml). This is the density of water. Because the density of water (1.0 g/ml) is used as a standard, densities of other liquids and solids can be compared to water. One source of student error will be in placing exactly 25 ml of water into the cup. You may wish to use a red marker to color the 25 ml line on the medicine cup. If available, a 25 ml graduated cylinder can be used and will increase the accuracy of measurement. Different solutions have different densities. Solutions with densities less than 1.0 will float on water. Solutions with densities greater than 1.0 will sink in water.

ACTIVITY **12**

Find the Density of a Salt Solution

MATERIALS

water   salt
equal-arm balance   medicine dropper
mass weights   plastic medicine cup

WHAT TO DO

▼ Add 5 grams of salt to 10 ml of water in a medicine cup.
▼ Stir until the salt dissolves.

PREDICTING   **What do you predict will be the density of this salt solution?**

▼ Weigh an empty cup on the balance.

MEASURING	**What is the mass of the cup and the salt water solution?**
MEASURING	**What is the mass of the solution only?**
MEASURING	**What is the volume of the solution in milliliters (ml)?**
MEASURING	**What is the density of the salt solution?**
SUPPORTING	**What reasons can you give for any difference between the density of the solution you predicted and the density you calculated from your observations?**
PREDICTING	**Do you think your salt solution will float or sink in tap water?**
APPLYING	***Try it!***
OBSERVING	**What did you observe?**
APPLYING	**How can you make a solution having a density that is twice that of water?**
APPLYING	***Try it!***

▼ Describe how you made the solution. (*Communicating*)
▼ Look again at Activity 4.

VERIFYING	**What is the density of the salt water solution you made in Activity 4?**

TEACHER BACKGROUND INFORMATION

Assuming the volume doesn't change with the addition of the salt, the density of the salt solution would be 1.5 (15 grams/10 ml = 1.5 g/ml). The same volume of plain water would have a density of 1.0 (10 grams/10 ml = 1.0 g/ml). Students should infer that salt water is heavier (more dense) than tap water. To make a salt solution with a density of 2.0, students could add 25 grams of salt to 25 ml of plain water. The mass of the salt solution would be 50 grams (25 grams of salt and 25 grams of water); the volume would be 25 ml. The density of the solution is the mass (50 grams) divided by the volume (25 ml) = 2 grams/milliliter. In Activity 4, the mass (weight) of 15 ml water and 10 grams of salt is 25 grams. If the volume remains 15 ml, the density would be 25g/15 ml or 1.67 g/ml.

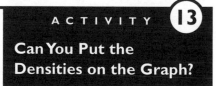

ACTIVITY 13

Can You Put the Densities on the Graph?

MATERIALS

data from activities 11 and 12   ruler
pencil   crayons

WHAT TO DO

COMMUNICATING	**What is the density of water?**

▼ On a graph (like the one below) mark a point showing the density of water.
▼ Mark points to show the densities of the other solutions (clear, red, green, and alcohol).
▼ Use a ruler to draw a line connecting each point to the 0 corner of the graph.
▼ Label each line on your graph showing which solution it is.

PREDICTING	**If you had a solution with a density of 4.0, where would the line go?**

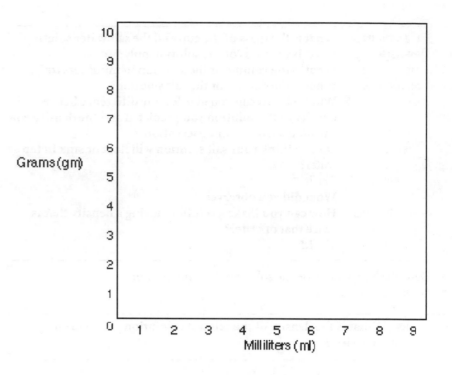

▼ Using a *yellow* crayon, color that part of your graph showing densities of any solutions that will sink in water. (*Categorizing*)
▼ Using a *red* crayon, color that part of your graph showing densities of any solutions that will *float* in water. (*Categorizing*)
▼ Pretend that you have a solution that has a density of 5 grams per milliliter.

COMMUNICATING   **How would you describe that solution to a friend?**

TEACHER BACKGROUND INFORMATION

You may want to review graphing skills with your students. The completed graph should be as seen below.

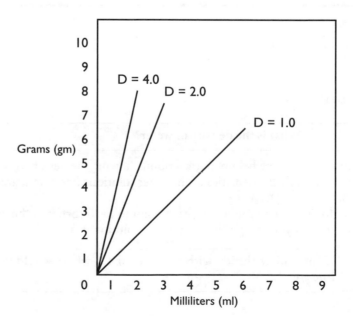

MATERIALS

balance   rubber stopper with hole
100 ml graduated cylinder   12-inch piece of string
beaker   water

WHAT TO DO

MEASURING	**Using a balance, what is the mass in grams of your rubber stopper?**
COMMUNICATING	**Record your measurement.**
HYPOTHESIZING	**How can you find the volume of an object like the rubber stopper?**

You can find the volume of the stopper by sinking it in water. When the stopper sinks, it pushes or *displaces* some of the water out of the way. The volume of the water displaced is equal to the volume of the stopper. A graduated cylinder can be used to measure how much water is displaced.

▼ Fill a 100-milliliter graduated cylinder with exactly 50 milliliters of water.
▼ Record the number of milliliters of water in the cylinder.
▼ Carefully drop your stopper into the cylinder.

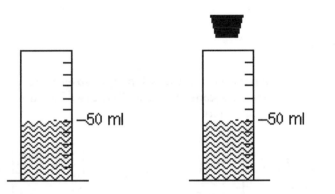

OBSERVING	**What happened to the level of the water in the cylinder?**
SUPPORTING	**What reasons can you give for your observation?**
MEASURING	**What is the new water level in the graduated cylinder?**

▼ Record your measurement. (*Communicating*)

VERIFYING	**How much water did the rubber stopper displace?**
OBSERVING	**What is the volume of your rubber stopper?**

▼ Record your measurement of the volume.
In Activity 11, you learned that the density of an object is a relationship between its mass and the volume it occupies.

VERIFYING	**Using the numbers you have obtained, what is the density of your rubber stopper?**

▼ Record the density you calculated. (*Communicating*)
▼ Using the graph from Activity 13, draw a line that stands for the density of your rubber stopper. (*Communicating*)

▼ Using the same procedures, find the density of other objects such as rocks, lead sinkers, and clay.

TEACHER BACKGROUND INFORMATION

The volume (in ml) of a solid can be found by measuring the volume of water displaced when the object is completely submerged in water. Therefore, students must calculate the difference in water levels before and after the object is placed in water. This can be most easily performed by using a graduated cylinder. Remember that to calculate the volume of an object that floats in water (wood, cork), the object must be totally submerged in the water to obtain the total volume of the object.

ACTIVITY **15**

The Great Root Beer Mystery

Teacher Demonstration

MATERIALS

two 1-gallon aquariums or any other similar containers
one 12-ounce unopened can of root beer
one 12-ounce unopened can of diet root beer (same brand)
equal-arm balance with mass weights
equipment necessary to measure volume of root beer cans
water

WHAT TO DO

PREDICTING   **What do you think will happen to each can of root beer when the cans are placed in the two half-filled aquariums or large jars?**

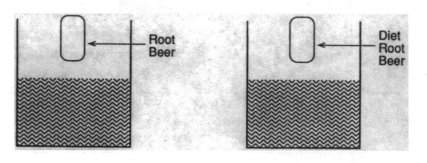

APPLYING   ***Try it!***
OBSERVING   **What did you observe?**
HYPOTHESIZING/ **What reasons can you give for any differences you**
RELATING   **observed in the behavior of the two cans?**
APPLYING   **How can you design an experiment to test your hypothesis?**

▼ Describe your experiment. (*Communicating*)
▼ Now Perform your experiment.

OBSERVING   **What did you observe?**
INFERRING   **What conclusion can you give for your observations?**
INFERRING   **What conclusion can you give for any differences in your observations between the can of root beer and the can of diet root beer?**

APPLYING	**What further experiments would you like to perform to test other hypotheses you have?**
PREDICTING	**What difference do you think you would observe between a can of Coke and a can of diet Coke?**
APPLYING	***Try it!***
OBSERVING	**What did you observe?**
INFERRING	**What conclusion can you give for your observations?**

TEACHER BACKGROUND INFORMATION

When the two cans are placed in the two aquariums or large jars of water, students should observe that the can of root beer sinks while the can of diet root beer floats. Students might hypothesize that the two solutions are different, e.g. one is more dense than the other. As a result, the can of diet root beer would float on the more dense solution. Students can easily design an experiment to test this hypothesis. Students will infer that the can of root beer is more dense than the can of diet root beer. Students should be encouraged to determine the density of both cans. They should recall the formula, $D = M/V$. Using their equal-arm balance, students can determine the mass of each can. They can determine the volume of each can either by water displacement or by measuring the dimensions of the can and using the formula, $V = \pi r^2 \times h$. Volume $= \pi$ (pi) $\times r^2$ (radius of can in centimeters) $\times h$ (height of can in centimeters). Students should discuss what tests they want to perform on the unopened cans and opened cans before opening the cans. Given granulated sugar, students could determine how much sugar was added to the can to account for the density of the root beer. If aspartame is available, the same could be done for the diet root beer.

ACTIVITY 16

What is the Density of an Egg?

MATERIALS

graduated cylinder (large enough for an egg to fit inside)
equal-arm balance with mass weights

egg   water
salt

WHAT TO DO

| HYPOTHESIZING | **What is the density of an egg?** |
| APPLYING | **How can you design an investigation to find out?** |

▼ Describe your investigation. (*Communicating*)

| VERIFYING | **Conduct your investigation. What is the density of your egg?** |
| PREDICTING | **To make the egg float in salt water, how dense must the salt water solution be?** |

▼ Now make a salt water solution having the density that you identified above.

| OBSERVING | **What did you observe when you placed your egg in the salt water solution?** |
| INFERRING | **What conclusion can you give for your observation?** |

▼ Remember what you discovered about the sinking and floating eggs in Activity 6.

SUPPORTING   **Explain why the egg sank in plain tap water in Activity 6.**

TEACHER BACKGROUND INFORMATION

This activity can provide an excellent opportunity to evaluate students' ability to calculate the density of both solids and liquids.

ACTIVITY **17**

Activity I Revisited: What New Ideas Do You Have?

Teacher Demonstration

MATERIALS

none, unless the demonstration is to be repeated (see Activity 1)

WHAT TO DO

▼ Draw a picture of the demonstration (or set it up live). (*Communicating*)

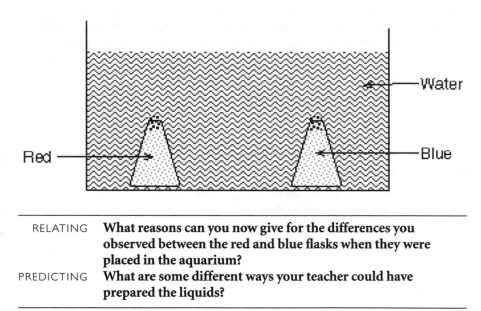

RELATING   **What reasons can you now give for the differences you observed between the red and blue flasks when they were placed in the aquarium?**

PREDICTING   **What are some different ways your teacher could have prepared the liquids?**

TEACHER BACKGROUND INFORMATION

This activity should be used as a wrap-up to pull together the major ideas of the unit. It could also be used as an evaluative tool to help you diagnose both the students' understanding of the activities performed and your teaching of the unit. Wait until all possible ways of preparing the solutions have been identified by the students during this discussion (differences in densities of the red and blue solutions and the aquarium water possibly caused by use of salt, alcohol, and so on) before reaching closure. Any major gaps you identify that are held by a sizable number of students should be closely examined for future teaching of the unit.

APPLYING THE LEARNING CYCLE STRATEGY TO A NEW TOPIC

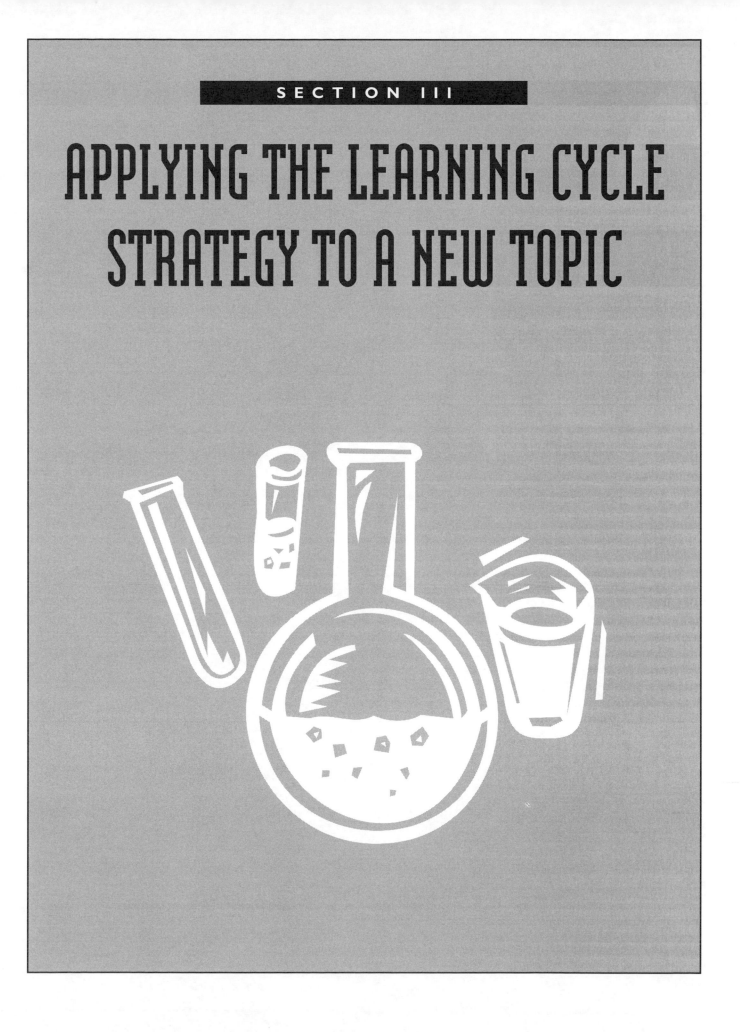

Surface Tension

▼

CONCEPT: *Surface tension is the attraction of like molecules on the surface of a liquid. Molecules of different liquids produce different amounts of surface tension.*

SPECIAL NOTE: *To develop a Learning Cycle on surface tension, you are encouraged to place the 14 activities below into a sequence where some activities precede the introduction of the concept (Exploration) and some follow the concept introduction (Application).*

NOTE: *The Learning Cycle sequence below will be determined by the activities you select for the Exploration and Application phases, and where you plan to introduce the concept.*

1 How fast does your boat move?

2 How can you make a dry spot?

3 What do drops look like?

4 Can toothpicks act like magnets?

5 How can you slip a coin between two wine glasses without getting wet? (Teacher Demonstration)

6 How full is full?

7 How many pennies will your cup hold?

8 How can you make a vegetable basket float?

9 How can you turn five streams of water into one?

10 How many drops can you place on a penny?

11 Which liquids make the best drops?

12 Which cup is the fullest?

13 How can you explain the mystery of the magic finger? (Student Demonstration)

14 How can you make a "nylon stocking" hold water in a jar?

SUGGESTED LEARNING CYCLE SEQUENCE

Exploration Activities:

Concept Introduction:

Application Activities:

INTRODUCTION

Cohesion is a force that tends to hold a liquid together because of the attraction of like or similar molecules. A concept closely related to cohesion is *surface tension*, the attraction of like molecules on the surface of a liquid. Molecules of different liquids produce different amounts of surface tension.

Molecules of water in comparison with other liquids—like soapy water or alcohol—have a strong attraction to each other. As a result, water demonstrates a high surface tension. The molecules of water at the surface are strongly attracted to each other forming a thin film, or "skin." Beneath the surface of the water, the water molecules are pulled equally in all directions by neighboring water molecules. On the surface of the water, there is no force to "pull" the water molecules upward; rather, many water molecules are pulling down and are squeezed together. Thus, the result is a downward force that accounts for the surface tension effect. This explains, for example, why water "heaps" higher than other liquids (Activities: "Which Cup is the Fullest?" "How Many Drops Can You Place on a Penny?"); forms more spherical drops (Activity, "What Do Drops Look Like?"); and forms larger drops (Activity, "Which Liquids Make the Biggest Drops?"). The difference in the surface tension among different liquids helps to explain the observations that students make in activities in this Learning Cycle topic. The use of liquid detergent serves to break the cohesive attraction forces among the water molecules, and thus weakens the surface tension of water.

In this series of activities, there are fourteen activities related to the concept of *surface tension*. The activities have been sequenced *randomly*. Unlike the Learning Cycle sequences in Section II of this book, these 14 activities have NOT been placed into a Learning Cycle sequence. This collection of activities was placed in Section III to allow you to apply the Learning Cycle strategy to the teaching of a new concept—surface tension. Your task is to develop a Learning Cycle sequence that is most consistent with your own logic of how the concept of surface tension should be presented to your children. Needless to say, if this task were given to 100 teachers, there would be at least 100 *different* Learning Cycle sequences—each consistent with each teacher's experiences, personality, and logic. Thus, the only right sequence is one that is consistent with the interests and needs of you and your students.

In developing a Learning Cycle sequence similar to those presented earlier, you must ask yourself a number of questions. How many activities do you want to include in your Learning Cycle? Do you want to identify additional activities and experiences from other sources? How many activities should you initially place in the Exploration Phase? Where should the Concept Introduction occur? How many activities should you place in the Application Phase? At this point you should perhaps reread the part from Section I on how to develop a Learning Cycle. Before you start you should take some time and read the fourteen activities that follow.

Included among the 14 activities are two clusters of activities: (*a*) those that involve a comparison of "heaping" in different liquids and drops of different liquids; and (*b*) those that involve a "pushing or pulling" of objects on the surface of the water. Each of these clusters could be developed in a number of ways within your Learning Cycle sequence.

With the large number of available activities in this Learning Cycle topic, you have a number of different options as you plan and implement your Learning Cycle sequence with your students. As you proceed, you must be sensitive to how well your students are grasping the concept. If, for example, you feel your students are progressing well and do not need all of the activities you placed in the Exploration Phase prior to the introduction of the concept, you might incorporate the unused activities either in the Application Phase or as evaluation items to assess their understanding of the concept.

ANALYSIS OF TEACHER QUESTIONS

In examining activities from each of the Learning Cycle sequences found in Section II, you observed that each activity contains a number of science process core questions. Questions are labeled in parentheses representing one of the science processes described in Section I. In the series of 14 activities related to surface tension found in Section III, notice that the science process core questions within each activity have NOT been classified. To more accurately classify each question, knowledge of the context of the question within the Learning Cycle sequence is necessary. Since the 14 activities are randomly organized, a Learning Cycle sequence does not exist. When you have organized the activities into your own Learning Cycle sequence, you will then have the opportunity to gain experience in categorizing the questions within each activity into their appropriate science processes. In addition, you should closely examine the questions provided for each activity and modify them to match your own logic and objectives for the activity. You will also need to add questions asking your students to compare observations and attributes among activities in your sequence.

SAFETY

Although the materials used in this sequence are relatively safe, children should be reminded *not* to taste any liquids without your permission.

Materials: The following materials needed in the

teaching of this Learning Cycle can be purchased from science supply companies such as Delta Education, P.O. Box M, Nashua, NH 03601–6012 (1–800–258–1302): Plastic dropper bottles, medicine droppers, medicine cups, 25 ml graduate cylinders.

REFERENCES

Adibe, N. 1983. "How Many Pennies Will a Glass of Water Hold?" *Science and Children* 20 (8): 52–53.

Blume, S.C., and Beisenherz, P.C. 1987. "Turning Your Class On to Cohesion." *Science and Children* 24 (7): 20–22.

Bubble-Ology: Teacher's Guide. 1986. Great Explorations in Math & Science (GEMS). Berkeley, CA: Lawrence Hall of Science, University of California.

Donalson-Sams, M. 1988. "Surface Tension: The Ways of Water." *Science and Children* 26 (3): 26–28.

Kitchen Physics: A Look at Some Properties of Liquids— Teacher's Guide. 1986. Elementary Science Study Series. Nashua, NH: Delta Education, Inc.

Liquids: Teacher's Guide. 1991. Insights. Newton, MA: Education Development Center, Inc.

Looking at Liquids: Teacher's Guide (1988). A Delta Science Module. Nashua, NH.

Lowery, L. 1985. *The Everyday Science Sourcebook: Ideas For Teaching in the Elementary/Middle School*. Palo Alto, CA: Dale Seymour Publications.

Marson, R. 1978. *Cohesion/Adhesion: A Task Card Module*. Task Oriented Physical Science (TOPS). Canby, OR: TOPS Learning Systems.

Mooney, P.A. 1989. "Science in Living Color." *Science and Children* 26 (5): 30–31.

Ward, A. 1981. "Pouring Water Sideways along a Wet String." *Science and Children* 18 (4): 26.

Wiebe, A. 1990. *Soap Films and Bubbles: Teacher's Guide*. 1990. Project AIMS. Fresno, CA: AIMS Education Foundation.

ACTIVITY 1

How Fast Does Your Boat Move?

MATERIALS

one small sheet of styrofoam (such as a discarded meat tray)

scissors   liquid detergent
alcohol

WHAT TO DO

▼ Cut the styrofoam into a rectangle, 7 centimeters long and 4 centimeters wide.

▼ Cut off the corners of one end of the rectangle.

▼ Cut a small slot in the center of the other end. See the picture below.

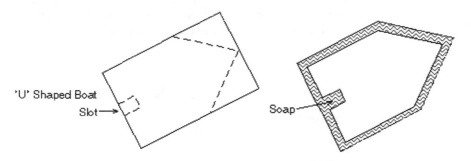

'U' Shaped Boat
Slot →   Soap →

▼ Fill a shallow pan with water, and wait until the water is still.

▼ Gently float the styrofoam "boat" on the water.

What will happen to the "boat" when a drop of liquid soap is put into the slot?
Try it!
What did you observe?
What reason can you give for your observation?
How fast does your "boat" move?

▼ Place another drop of soap into the slot.

What happened to the "boat" this time?
What reasons can you give for any differences you observed?

▼ Rinse all the soap from the pan and the boat.

How will a drop of alcohol affect your "boat"?
Try it!
Was the movement of the "boat" a result of a push or a pull?
What reasons can you give for your answer?

TEACHER BACKGROUND INFORMATION:

As the liquid detergent (or alcohol) reduces the surface tension inside the slot and behind the "boat," the higher surface tension of the water in front of the boat "pulls" it forward. Placing a second drop of soap in the slot will not result in as much movement of the "boat" because the surface tension of the water has been lessened significantly by the first drop.

ACTIVITY 2

How Can You Make a Dry Spot?

MATERIALS

clean glass microscope slide or small flat plate

food coloring	medicine dropper
water	alcohol
liquid detergent	

WHAT TO DO

▼ Lay a clean microscope slide on a piece of white paper on a flat, level surface.
▼ Using your medicine dropper, cover the top of the slide with a thin layer of colored water.

What will happen to the colored water when 1 or 2 drops of alcohol are added to the center of the slide?
Try it!

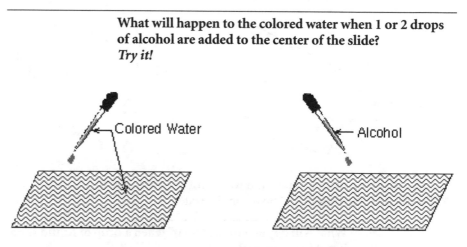

What did you observe?
What reasons can you give for any changes you observed?
Was the movement you observed a result of a push or a pull?
What reason can you give for your answer?

What other substances could you add to the colored water
to produce the same changes?
Try it!

TEACHER BACKGROUND INFORMATION:

Students should observe that when one or two drops of alcohol hit the surface of the
colored water, the colored water quickly moves away, leaving a dry spot. The alcohol
reduces the surface tension in the immediate area of the drop. The plain-colored
water still possesses a strong surface tension. Thus, the colored water is "pulled"
from the region of the alcohol drop (the region of lowered surface tension).

What Do Drops Look Like?

MATERIALS

waxed paper   alcohol
three medicine droppers water
toothpicks   soapy water

WHAT TO DO

▼ Place a few drops of each liquid—water, alcohol, and soapy water—on three
   separate pieces of waxed paper.
▼ Draw the shape of each drop.
▼ Describe the shape of the drops of each liquid.

   How are the drops alike?
   How are they different?

▼ See if you can lead the drops around on the waxed paper with your pencil.
▼ Put the tip of your pencil into the middle of the drop and try to pull it.

   How many drops can you pull at one time?
   Try it!
   What happens when the drops get too close to each other?
   What reasons can you give for your observations?

TEACHER BACKGROUND INFORMATION

The greater surface tension of water tends to pull the drops into spheres. Drops
of alcohol and soapy water will tend to be flatter.

Can Toothpicks Act like Magnets?

MATERIALS

two toothpicks   pan or bowl
medicine dropper   water
liquid detergent   alcohol

WHAT TO DO

▼ Put one toothpick on the surface of the water.
▼ Put the other one next to the first toothpick, about the width of a toothpick
   apart.

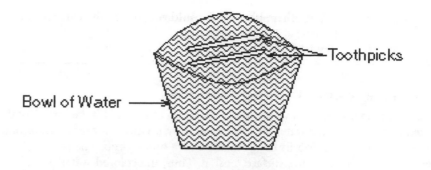

What happens to the toothpicks in the water?

What will happen if you put a drop of detergent into the water *between* the toothpicks?

Try it!

What reasons can you give for your observation?

How would your observations be different if you used alcohol instead of soap?

Try it! (Be sure to clean the toothpicks and use fresh water.)

How were your observations with the toothpicks like the behavior of two magnets placed together? How were they different?

Was the movement of the toothpicks the result of a push or a pull?

What reasons can you give for your answer?

TEACHER BACKGROUND INFORMATION

The toothpicks moved away from each other (separated) when a drop of liquid detergent was added because the soap reduced the surface tension between the toothpicks. The surface tension of the plain water on the outside of the toothpicks served to pull the toothpicks away from each other. Students using alcohol instead of the soap will make the same observations.

ACTIVITY **5**

How Can You Slip a Coin Between Two Wine Glasses Without Getting Wet?

Teacher Demonstration

MATERIALS

two identical clean wine glasses

deep bowl or sink of water   dime or quarter
flat surface

WHAT TO DO

▼ Hold the two glasses under water, until they are filled with water.

▼ Then, keeping them under water, turn one upside down exactly on top of the other (see picture A below).

▼ Carefully remove the glasses from the water in the same position.

▼ Place them on a flat surface (see picture B below).

▼ One glass should be upside down and on top of the other.

▼ Both glasses should be completely filled with water.

What do you think will happen if you place a coin between the two glasses (see picture C below)?

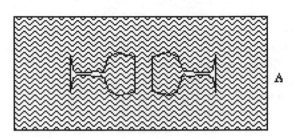

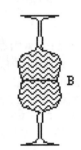

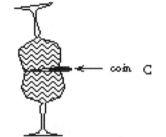

▼ Now carefully tilt the top glass slightly, just enough so that you can place the coin through the narrow gap between the two glasses.
▼ The coin should remain between the two glasses.

What happened to the water when the coin was placed between the two glasses?
What reasons can you give for your observations?
Do you think you can use a quarter instead of a dime and produce the same results?
Try it!

TEACHER BACKGROUND INFORMATION

Surface tension enables the surface of water to behave like a skin or film. This film prevents the water from flowing through the gap between the glasses created by the insertion of the dime.

ACTIVITY 6

How Full Is Full?

MATERIALS

water (may be colored with food coloring)
30 ml plastic medicine cup or baby food jar

medicine dropper   paper towels

WHAT TO DO

▼ Place medicine cup on a paper towel.
▼ Carefully fill the cup to the very top with water.
▼ Keep the outside of the cup as dry as possible.
▼ Using your medicine dropper, carefully add more water to the cup.
▼ Stop when the water just begins to spill over the side of the cup.
▼ Draw a picture of how the water looked just before it spilled over.

What reasons can you give for your observation?

TEACHER BACKGROUND INFORMATION

The water will significantly "heap" or stick together over the top of the cup before it spills. The top will be dome-shaped. The "stickiness" that holds the water together is called surface tension (from the Latin *teneo* meaning *to hold*). Molecules of water are held together so the cup can be filled more than full. Once this surface tension is broken, the water will not hold together as well.

ACTIVITY 7

How Many Pennies Will Your Cup Hold?

MATERIALS

large number of pennies (or washers, paper clips)
large container or tray for overflow

paper towels   container of water
two baby food jars or cups

WHAT TO DO

▼ Fill one baby food jar as full as you can with water. Fill the jar just to the point of spilling over.
▼ Keep the outside of the cup dry.
▼ Add pennies, one by one, to the jar until the water first spills over.

HINT: Drop the pennies gently into the cup without touching the sides of the cup or splashing the water.

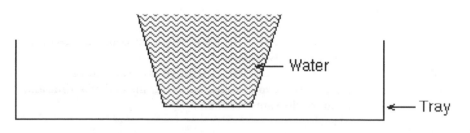

How many pennies do you think the jar will hold before it overflows?
Try it!
What did you observe?

▼ Now do the same activity using *soapy* water instead of plain water.

How many pennies do you predict the soapy water cup will
hold?

What did you observe?

What reasons can you give for any differences you
observed?

TEACHER BACKGROUND INFORMATION

A larger number of pennies may be added to a liquid possessing greater surface
tension. Therefore, students will observe that many more pennies can be added
to a jar of water than to a jar of soapy water or alcohol. If a smaller container is
used such as a 30 ml cup, paper clips or small washers could be used in place of
the pennies. Be sure that your students fill the jar just to the point of spilling *before* adding the pennies.

ACTIVITY   8

How Can You Make a Vegetable Basket Float?

MATERIALS

water	large container
plastic vegetable basket	liquid detergent

WHAT TO DO

▼ Fill the container with water.

What will happen when you carefully try to float the
vegetable basket on the surface of the water?

Try it!

What reasons can you give for your observation?

What will happen if you push on the corner of the basket
with your finger?

Try it!

What did you observe?

What reasons can you give for your observation?

How else could you sink the basket without touching it?

Try it!

What did you observe?

What reasons can you give for your observation?

HINT: Place the basket flat on
the surface of still water.

TEACHER BACKGROUND INFORMATION

Surface tension enables the vegetable basket to float on the surface of the water.
Adding a few drops of liquid detergent will lower the surface tension and cause
the basket to sink.

ACTIVITY   9

How Can You Make a Circle with a Thread?

MATERIALS

pan or bowl	water
medicine dropper	liquid detergent
alcohol	thread (nonabsorbent)
thin rubber band	

WHAT TO DO

▼ Tie the ends of a piece of thread together to make a loop.
▼ Place the thread loop on top of the water in your bowl.

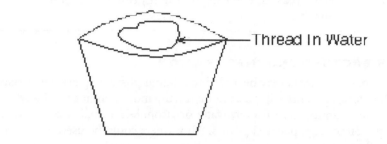
—Thread In Water

How can you change the shape into a circle without touching the thread?
Try it!
Describe your experiment.
What did you observe?
What reasons can you give for your observation?
Was the movement of the thread a result of a push or a pull?
What reason can you give for your answer?

▼ Place a thin, flexible rubber band on top of a *clean* bowl of water.

How can you change the shape of the rubber band into a circle without touching the thread?
Try it!

TEACHER BACKGROUND INFORMATION

The drop of liquid detergent added to water inside the loop of thread reduces the surface tension inside the loop. Since the surface tension of the plain water outside the loop is still strong, the thread will be pulled out into a circle. Try this activity prior to performing it in class. Try different kinds of thread to find one that works. Have students try different kinds of rubber bands to find one that will float and will form a circle when a drop of liquid detergent or alcohol is placed in the center of the rubber band.

ACTIVITY **10**

How Can You Turn Five Streams of Water into One?

MATERIALS

one empty 2-liter plastic soda bottle with screw cap

| nail | hammer |
| water | sink or empty bucket |

WHAT TO DO

▼ With a hammer and nail, make 5 holes very near the bottom of the 2-liter soda bottle.
▼ The holes should be about 5 millimeters (mm) apart. (See the picture below.)

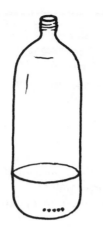

▼ Fill the bottle with water and screw the cap on the bottle. Hold the bottle over a sink or bucket.

▼ Unscrew the cap until you observe the water coming from the bottle in five streams. (See the picture below.)

▼ Now try to pinch the streams together with your thumb and forefinger.

What do you think will happen to the five streams?
What did you observe?
What reasons can you give for your observations?

TEACHER BACKGROUND INFORMATION

Students should observe that when the five streams are pinched, one stream is produced. When a student rubs his or her hand across the holes in the can, the stream of water will again flow in five separate streams. The strong attraction of the water molecules to each other causes five streams to come together into one stream. Rubbing a hand across the single stream breaks the surface tension and produces the five streams.

ACTIVITY 11

How Many Drops Can You Place on a Penny?

MATERIALS

pennies
three small cups
3 medicine droppers
paper towels

water
soapy water
alcohol

WHAT TO DO

▼ Fill three small cups with water, soapy water, and alcohol.
▼ Fill the medicine dropper with water from the cup with water.
▼ Carefully place drops of the water on a penny.
▼ Count the drops.

> **How many drops of water do you think the penny will hold before the water flows over the side of the penny? *Try it!***

▼ Record the number of drops in a chart like the one below.
▼ Repeat the experiment two more times and record your results.

> **What do you observe about the drops of water on the penny?**

▼ Now do the same activity using *soapy water* instead of plain water.
▼ First, predict how many drops of soapy water the penny will hold.
▼ Record the number of drops of soapy water in your chart.

> **Which penny held the most drops?**
> **What reasons can you give for your observations?**

▼ Now do the same activity using *alcohol*.
▼ Add drops of alcohol to the penny until the alcohol flows over the side.
▼ Record the number of drops of alcohol in your chart.

> **Which penny held the most drops?**
> **What reasons can you give for your observations?**

LIQUID	DROPS PREDICTED	DROPS ADDED TO PENNY		
		1st Trial	2nd Trial	3rd Trial
WATER				
SOAPY WATER				
ALCOHOL				
SUGAR				

> **What variables did you control in your experiment?**
> **What variables did you *not* control in your experiment?**

TEACHER BACKGROUND INFORMATION

Because of the higher surface tension of water, water should "heap" higher on the penny than the other liquids. Because of differences in drop size among the three liquids (see another of the 14 activities), differences in the number of drops on the pennies among the three liquids before the water overflows might not be as great as expected. It is important for students to control as many variables as possible; for example, penny, side of penny, condition of penny (old/new, clean/dirty), medicine dropper, angle at which the medicine dropper is held.

ACTIVITY **12**

Which Liquids Make the Biggest Drops?

MATERIALS

container of water
container of alcohol
medicine dropper

container of soapy water
10 ml graduated cylinder

WHAT TO DO

▼ Using your medicine dropper, carefully place 100 drops of plain water into a 10 ml graduated cylinder.

▼ Draw a picture of a graduated cylinder and mark on it a line that matches the amount of water in your cylinder.

▼ Record the number of milliliters (ml) in a chart like the one below.

▼ Clean and dry the cylinder and medicine dropper.

▼ Repeat the experiment using *soapy* water instead of plain water.

▼ Draw another graduated cylinder that matches the amount of soapy water in your cylinder.

▼ Record the number of milliliters (ml) in your chart.

▼ Clean and dry the cylinder and medicine dropper. Repeat the experiment using alcohol.

▼ Record your observations.

LIQUID	NUMBER OF ML
WATER	
SOAPY WATER	
ALCOHOL	

Which cylinder of 100 drops held the most liquid?
Which cylinder of 100 drops held the least liquid?
What reasons can you give for any differences you observed?
Which liquid had the biggest drops?
How did you know?
Why did you use the *same* medicine dropper for all four liquids?

TEACHER BACKGROUND INFORMATION

As water has greater surface tension, students should observe that water should make bigger drops, yielding more water than soapy water per 100 drops. Because of the variability in drop size among medicine droppers, the same medicine dropper should be used for all three liquids.

ACTIVITY 13

Which Cup Is the Fullest?

MATERIALS

four 30 ml medicine cups or baby food jars
four medicine droppers (or fewer, if they can be washed)

water	soapy water
alcohol	paper towels

WHAT TO DO

▼ Place your cups on paper toweling.
▼ Using the materials listed, fill your cups as full as you can with each liquid.
▼ Use a clean medicine dropper and add drops of the same liquid to each cup.
▼ Stop just as each cup spills.
▼ Draw a top on each of the cups below to show what the top of each cup looked like just before it spilled.

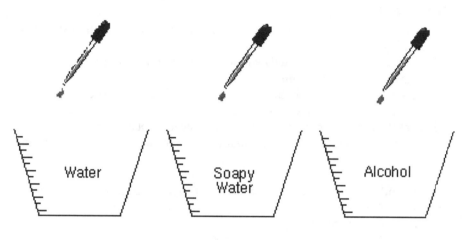

What differences did you observe among the cups?
What reasons can you give for your observations?

TEACHER BACKGROUND INFORMATION

Students should observe that water "heaps" the most as it has the strongest surface tension. Soapy water and alcohol will "heap" significantly less as there is less attraction among the molecules at the surface of the liquid.

ACTIVITY 14

How Can You Explain the Mystery of the Magic Finger?

Student Demonstration

MATERIALS

large bowl	water
pepper	liquid detergent

WHAT TO DO

▼ Secretly have one child rub some liquid detergent on his or her fingertip before returning to class. Send him or her on a small errand to do this.

▼ When the child returns, have another student sprinkle pepper on the surface of water in a large bowl.

What will happen when someone puts his or her finger into the water?
What did you observe?
Who can stick a finger into the water and not get pepper on that finger?

▼ Have other students try. They should all have pepper on their fingers.
▼ Now let the "special" student raise his hand and try. The class should observe the pepper moving quickly away from his finger. His finger will be free of pepper.

What reasons can you give for your observation?

TEACHER BACKGROUND INFORMATION

When the students place their fingers in the water, the pepper will stick to their fingers. When a finger coated with liquid detergent (unknown to the rest of the class) is placed in the water, the pepper is repelled and the pepper does not adhere to the finger. This is due to the lowered surface tension in the water around the soapy finger. Actually, the pepper is being "pulled" by the surface tension of the water farther away from the contact with the soap. This activity can provide an excellent discrepant event for students.

MATERIALS

jar	nylon stocking
water	soapy water
rubber band or string	alcohol
pail	

ACTIVITY 15
How Can You Make a "Nylon Stocking" Hold Water in a Jar?

WHAT TO DO

▼ Cut a square of nylon stocking about twice the size of the opening of the jar.
▼ Place the square over the top of the jar.
▼ Use a rubber band or string to hold the nylon to the jar.
▼ Fill the jar with water by pouring the water through the nylon.

What do you think will happen to the water in the jar when you turn the jar upside down?

▼ Try it by placing your hand over the mouth of the jar and turning the jar upside down.
▼ Then remove your hand from the mouth of the jar.

What did you observe?
What reasons can you give for your observation?
How would the results with soapy water and alcohol compare with your results with water?
Try it!

TEACHER BACKGROUND INFORMATION

Students will make the puzzling observation that they can pour water into the jar with the nylon "lid" but the water will not come out as easily when the jar is quickly inverted. The water molecules forming a film (surface tension) on the nylon lid enable the water to stay in the jar with the aid of atmospheric pressure. Soapy water has less surface tension and can be more easily poured out of the jar.

Additional Resources for Science Teachers

Abruscato, J., and Hassard, J., 1991. *The Whole Cosmos Catalog of Science Activities,* 2nd ed. Glenview, IL: Scott, Foresman and Company.

Ardley, N., et al. 1984. *How Things Work.* New York: Simon and Schuster, Inc.

Bennett, J. 1989. *Bright Ideas Science.* New York: Scholastic Publications Ltd.

Bosak, S.V. 1991. *Science Is...* Richmond Hill, Ontario, Canada: Scholastic Canada Ltd.

Brown, R.J. 1984. *333 Science Tricks and Experiments.* Blue Ridge Summit, PA: TAB Books, Inc.

Brown, R.J. 1984. *333 More Science Tricks and Experiments.* Blue Ridge Summit, PA: TAB Books, Inc.

Brown, R.J. 1987. *200 Illustrated Science Experiments for Children.* Blue Ridge Summit, PA: TAB Books, Inc.

Brown, R.J. 1988. *More Science for You: 112 Illustrated Experiments.* Blue Ridge Summit, PA: TAB Books, Inc.

Cash, T. 1993. *101 Physics Tricks.* New York: Sterling Publishing Company.

Cash, T., Parker, S., and Taylor, B. 1989. *175 More Science Experiments to Amuse and Amaze Your Friends.* New York: Random House.

Chapman, P. 1976. *The Young Scientist Book of Electricity.* Published in USA by EDC Publishing.

Churchill, E.R. 1992. *Amazing Science Experiments with Everyday Materials.* New York: Sterling Publishing Company.

Cobb, V. 1985. *Chemically Active! Experiments You Can Do at Home.* New York: Harper & Row.

DeVito, A., and Krockover, G.H. 1991. *Creative Sciencing.* Glenview, IL: Scotts, Foresman and Company.

DeVito, A. 1989. *Creative Wellsprings for Science Teaching,* 2nd ed. West Lafayette, IN: Creative Ventures Inc.

Freeman, I.M. Revised by W.J. Durden. 1990. *Physics Made Simple.* New York: Doubleday.

Friedl, A.E. 1991. *Teaching Science to Children—An Integrated Approach,* 2nd ed. New York: McGraw-Hill, Inc.

Funk, H.J., Fiel, R.L., Okey, J.R., Jaus, H.H., and Sprague, C.S. 1985. *Learning Science Process Skills.* Dubuque, IO: Kendall/ Hunt Publishing Company.

Gega, P.C. 1989. *Science in Elementary Education,* 6th ed. New York: Macmillan Publishing Company.

Hall, M.Y. 1988. *Simple Science Experiences.* Instructor Handbook Series.

Hann, J. 1991. *How Science Works.* Pleasantville, NY: Reader's Digest Association.

Hassard, J. 1990. *Science Experiences—Cooperative Learning and the Teaching of Science.* Menlo Park, CA: Addison-Wesley Publishing Company.

Hebert, D. 1968. *Mr. Wizzard's 400 Experiments in Science.* Revised by David Goldberg 1983. 500 74th Street, North Bergen, NJ 07047: Book Lab.

Hone, E., et al. 1971. *A Sourcebook for Elementary Science,* 2nd ed. New York: Harcourt Brace, Publishers.

Johnson, D.W., Johnson, R.T., and Holubec, E.J. 1991. *Cooperation in the Classroom.* 7208 Cornelia Drive, Edina, MN 55435: Interaction Book Company.

Kramer, A. 1989. *How to Make a Chemical Volcano and Other Mysterious Experiments.* New York: Franklin Watts Company.

Krishnan, C.V. 1990. *Physics Hands-On Activities.* 1910 Hidden Point Rd., Annapolis, MD 21401-9720: Alpha Publishing Company, Inc.

Levenson, E. 1985. *Teaching Children about Science.* New York: Prentice-Hall Press.

Levy, S.S. 1990. *Physical Science Hands-On Activities.* 1910 Hidden Point Rd., Annapolis, MD 21401-9720: Alpha Publishing Company, Inc.

Liem, T. 1990. *Invitations to Science Inquiry.* Chino Hills, CA: Science Inquiry Enterprises.

Lowery, L. 1985. *The Everyday Science Sourcebook-Ideas for Teaching in the Elementary/Middle School.* Palo Alto, CA: Dale Seymour Publications.

Lunetta, V., and Novick, S. 1982. *Inquiry and Problem Solving in the Physical Sciences: A Sourcebook.* Dubuque, IO: Kendall-Hunt Publishing Company.

Mandell, M. 1989. *Simple Science Experiments with Everyday Materials.* New York: Sterling Publishing Company, Inc.

McGill, O. 1984. *Science Magic: 101 Experiments You Can Do.* New York: Arco Publishing, Inc.

Munson, H.R. 1988. *Science Experiences with Everyday Things.* Belmont, CA: Fearon Teacher Aids.

Nelson, L.W., and Lorbeer, G.C. 1984. *Science Activities for Elementary Children.* Dubuque, IO: William C. Brown Publishers.

Osborne, R., and Freyberg, P. 1985. *Learning in Science— The Implications of Children's Science.* Portsmouth, NH: Heinemann.

Ostlund, K.L. 1992. *Science Process Skills: Assessing Hands-On Student Performance.* Menlo Park, CA: Addison-Wesley Publishing Company.

Schneider, M.S. 1980. *Science Projects for the Intermediate Grades.* Carthage, IL: Fearon Teacher Aids.

Strongin, H. 1992. *Science on a Shoestring,* 2nd ed. Palo Alto, CA: Dale Seymour Publications.

The Thomas Alva Edison Foundation. 1988. *The Thomas Edison Book of Easy and Incredible Experiments.* New York: John Wiley & Sons.

Tolman, M.N., and Morton, J.O. 1986. *Physical Science Activities for Grades 2–8.* West Nyack, NY: Parker Publishing Company, Inc.

Van Cleave, J. 1989. *Chemistry for Every Kid.* New York: John Wiley & Sons, Inc.

Van Cleave, J. 1991. *Physics for Every Kid.* New York: John Wiley & Sons, Inc.

Walpole, B. 1988. *175 Science Experiments to Amuse and Amaze Your Friends.* New York: Random House.

Williams, R.A., Rockwell, R.E., and Sherwood, E.A. 1987. *Mudpies to Magnets.* Mt. Rainier, MD: Gryphon House, Inc.

Wood, R.W. 1989. *Physics for Kids—49 Easy Experiments with Mechanics.* Blue Ridge Summit, PA: TAB Books, Inc.

ADDITIONAL SOURCES OF HANDS-ON ACTIVITIES

AIMS. Activities Integrating Mathematics and Science. AIMS Education Foundation, P.O. Box 8120, Fresno, CA 93747–8120, (209) 255–4094. Hands-on Enrichment Units Integrating Mathematics and Science.

Grades 5–9: *Math and Science, A Solution; The Sky's the Limit; From Head to Toe; Fun with Foods; Floaters and Sinkers; Down to Earth; Our Wonderful World; Pieces and Patterns, A Patchwork in Math and Science; Out of this World; Soap Films and Bubbles; Mostly Magnets; Electrical Connections.*

CHEM. Chemicals, Health, Environment, and Me. Lawrence Hall of Science, Berkeley, University of California, Berkeley, CA 94720, (415) 642–8718. Ten modules organized around chemistry topics for grades 5 and 6: *Everyday Chemicals; My Sweet Tooth; Mystery Spill; Hazardous Home; Trash or Cash; The Inside Story; What is a Threshold; Smoking and My Health; Update of Hazardous Home: Carbon Dioxide and Me.* Teacher guides and kit materials available from: Sargent Welch, VWR Scientific, 911 Commerce Court, Buffalo Grove, IL 60089–2375, 1–800–727–4368.

Free catalogs available for ESS Teacher Guides, SAPA II Teacher Guides, and Delta Science Modules for grades K–8. Delta Education, Inc., P.O. Box M, Nashua, NH 03061–6012, 1–800–258–1302.

Available Delta Science Modules for the Physical Sciences: *Investigating Water; Properties; Length and Capacity; Sink or Float; States of Matter; Electrical Circuits; Looking at Liquids; Measuring; Powders and Crystals; Sound; Color and Light; Electromagnetism; Lenses and Mirrors; Simple Machines.*

FOSS. Full Option Science System. Encyclopedia Britannica Education Corporation, Instructional Materials, 310 South Michigan Avenue, Chicago, IL 60604–9839, 1–800–554–9862. Use of direct, hands-on involvement in the physical, life, and earth sciences, for grades 3–6.

GEMS. Great Explorations in Math and Science. Lawrence Hall of Science, University of California, Berkeley, CA 94720, (510) 642–7771. Middle school hands-on math and science units include:

Grades 4–8: *Crime Lab Chemistry; Fingerprinting; Hot Water & Warm Homes; Of Cabbages and Chemistry; Oobleck: What Do Scientists Do?; Quadice; Vitamin C Testing.*

Grades 5–8: *Color Analyzers; Paper Towel Testing.*

Grades 5–9: *Bubble-Ology; Earth, Moon, and Stars; Mapping Animal Movements.*

Grades 6–9: *Animals in Action; Convection: A Current Event; More Than Magnifiers; River Cutters.*

Grades 6–10: *Chemical Reactions; Discovering Density; Earthworms; Experimenting with Model Rockets; Height-O-Meters; Mapping Fish Habitats; Acid Rain.*

Grades 7–10: *Global Warming and the Greenhouse Effect.*

INSIGHTS: Improving Urban Middle School Science. Education Development Center, Inc., 55 Chapel Street, Newton, MA 02160, (617) 969–7100, 1–800–225–4276. Teacher's guides and kit materials available from: Science Kit & Boreal Laboratories Elementary Science Division, 777 East Park Drive, Tonawanda, NY 14150–6784, 1–800–828–7777. Hands-On inquiry science curriculum units include:

Grades K–1: *Living Things; Balls and Ramps; Myself and Others; The Senses.*

Grades 2–3: *Habitats; Liquids: Growing Things; Lifting Heavy Things; Sound.*

Grades 4–5: *Bones and Skeletons; The Mysterious Powder; Changes of State; Circuits and Pathways; Reading the Environment.*

Grades 5–6: *Human Body Systems; Structures; There Is No Way.*

OPERATION PHYSICS. Physics Department, Louisiana State University, Baton Rouge, LA 70808. Project designed to improve the teaching and learning of basic physics concepts in the upper elementary and middle school grades. Topics include the following books: *Behavior of Light; Magnets and Magnetism; Measurement; Electricity; Heat; Sound; Matter and Its Changes; Forces and Motion; Energy; Color and Vision; Astronomy; Simple Machines; and Forces in Fluids.*

SAVI/SELPH. Science Activities for the Visually Impaired/ Science Enrichment for Learners with Physical Handicaps. Center for Multisensory Learning, Lawrence Hall of Science, Berkeley, CA 94720, (415) 642–8941.

Middle School units include:

Higher Level Modules: *Magnetism and Electricity; Mixtures and Solutions; Environments; Kitchen Interactions; Environmental Energy.*

SCIENCE AND TECHNOLOGY FOR CHILDREN. National Science Resources Center, Smithsonian Institution, National Academy of Sciences, Arts, and Industries Building, Room 1201, Washington, D.C. 20560. Teacher's guides and kit materials available from: Carolina Biological Supply Company, 2700 York Road, Box 187, Gladstone, OR 97027, 1–800–334–5551.

Middle school hands-on science units include:

Grade 4: *Electric Circuits; Ourselves; Animal Behavior; Floating and Sinking.*

Grade 5: *Microworlds; Ecosystems; Food Chemistry; Structures.*

Grade 6: *Experiments with Plants; Magnets and Motors; It's About Time; Machines and Inventions.*

SEPUP. Science Education for Public Understanding Program. Lawrence Hall of Science, University of California at Berkeley. Teacher's Guides and Kit Materials available from: Sargent-Welch, VWR Scientific, 911 Commerce Court, Buffalo Grove, IL 60089–2375, 1–800–727–4368.

Middle/ junior high school hands-on science modules include: *Chemical Survey & Solutions and Pollution; Groundwater: The Fruitvale Story; Toxic Waste: A Teaching Simulation; Plastics in Our Lives; Investigating Chemical Processes: Your Island Factory; Chemicals in Foods: Additives; The Waste Hierarchy: Where is "Away"?; Investigation of Hazardous Materials; Environmental Health Risks.*

TOPS. Task Oriented Physical Science learning systems. 10970 S. Mulino Road, Canby, OR 97013.

Open-ended TASK CARD modules in the physical sciences include: *Pendulums; Floating and Sinking; Analysis; Oxidation; Solutions; Cohesion/Adhesion; Kinetic Model; Heat; Pressure; Light; Sound; Electricity; Magnetism; Motion; Machines.*